INVESTING
WITHOUT BORDERS

INVESTING
WITHOUT BORDERS

How 6 Billion Investors
Can Find Profits
in the Global Economy

DANIEL FRISHBERG

WILEY

John Wiley & Sons, Inc.

Published by John Wiley & Sons, Inc., Hoboken, New Jersey.
Published simultaneously in Canada.

For general information on our other products and services or for technical support, please contact our Customer Care Department within the United States at (800) 762-2974, outside the United States at (317) 572-3993 or fax (317) 572-4002.

Wiley also publishes its books in a variety of electronic formats. Some content that appears in print may not be available in electronic books. For more information about Wiley products, visit our web site at www.wiley.com.

Library of Congress Cataloging-in-Publication Data:

Frishberg, Daniel, 1945–
    Investing without borders : how six billion investors can find profits in the global economy / Daniel Frishberg.
        p. cm.
    Includes index.
    ISBN 978-0-470-49649-7 (cloth)
    1. Investments, Foreign. 2. Investments. I. Title.
    HG4538.F74 2010
    332.6–dc22

                                                                                    2009043707

Printed in the United States of America

10 9 8 7 6 5 4 3 2 1

To Elisea, the love of my life–

When I became your husband, at age 40, I became a better man. It's just that simple. At every challenge and in every test, my strength, endurance, and courage comes from the fact that I am always playing for you.

Right from the beginning, you saw something in me that I couldn't see. You saw the power in me that I never saw in myself— always believing in me, steadily inspiring me to soar to heights I never dared imagine.

Your unlimited kindness and compassion, that unbelievable stability, your ability to generate life from inside you instead of reacting to events like the rest of us tend to do. You inspire me and that inspiration has given my life a meaning it never had before.

I won the lottery that day many years ago, when I held that door open for you and you looked up at me with that first smile that lit a fire that has never gone out.

The year we married you told me you saw gifts you had never seen before. You said you had never seen anyone before who really understood the stock market and who understood "where the money is."

You asked, "Why not spend this second half of your life sharing those gifts with the world."

I told you I didn't know how to do that, and you have spent the rest of your life showing me how.

To you, I dedicate this book and my life. Elisea, it's been quite a ride.

To Stephanie–

As I became your dad, I became a man. You have grown into a confident, gifted, beautiful, and vibrant human being. Growing up with you has been the greatest gift God could have bestowed on me. No one could ever take your place in my heart.

To Niki–

You have managed to forge a singular blend of discipline, confidence, humor, beauty, and talent. Your great journey is ahead of you, but already you blow me away with your inner strength and your tender heart. Whenever I watch you live your life, I cannot help but smile. I wish I was more like you.

To Larry–

I am proud to call you my son. You are but a child and already you amaze me with your ability to commit, your gentleness, your unbelievable talent and tenacity, and your natural ability to practice and master everything you try. I watch you and I think I must be a pretty good man to have helped to create a son like you.

Contents

Foreword

Who would have ever guessed, even as recently as early 2007, how quickly our economic and financial world could implode. The phrase "one in a million" seems apropos, but in truth financial crises and economic collapses occur frequently. And when they do occur, the world changes—and rarely for the better. Everyone in politics uses a crisis to push their favorite agenda. Think here of President Obama's Chief of Staff Rahm Emmanuel, who is reputed to have said that a good crisis should never be allowed to go to waste.

In the United States, the government has used this latest crisis to become an even larger participant than it already was in home mortgages, autos, banking, insurance, health care, and energy. To say that these industries have been nationalized would be an overreach, but not by much. The primary focus of private businesses today is definitely government relations. And who knows how far this nationalization trend will go? My suspicion is that it will go a lot further than it already has, and the economy will take a lot longer to become healthy, if it ever does.

We have lived in a predominantly competitive private enterprise capitalist economic environment since President Reagan took office. During this period from the late 1970s/early 1980s to the early 2000s, prosperity was the norm. The stock market in the U.S., for example, as represented by the Dow Jones Industrial Average rose from a low of below 800 in August of 1982 to a high above 14,000 in October of 2007. Even after allowing for inflation, this is an impressive record of appreciation.

To argue that this prosperity represented the ascendance of Republicans over Democrats or conservatives over liberals would be just plain wrong. Good economics knows no party label, nor for that matter does bad economics. It is true that President Reagan was a

ix

Republican, but Democratic President Clinton was arguably on a par with President Reagan. From my perspective, it would be hard to make a positive case for either Republican President Bush the elder or his son. It's not the party that matters; it's the economics.

The successes of Lady Thatcher, Ronald Reagan, and their successors were not confined to the territorial boundaries of the U.K. and the U.S. This world has changed as has rarely been seen in history. The communist behemoth formerly known as the evil empire of the U.S.S.R. collapsed before our very eyes, giving birth to wildly expansive entrepreneurial capitalist nations in Eastern Europe. Even Communist China morphed into one of the fastest growing supply-side nations this planet has ever known. In China alone, more people have been removed from poverty rolls than has occurred from the first human on earth until 1980 all combined. That really is something to brag about.

And then there were the successes of India, Viet Nam, South Korea, Ireland, Singapore, Chile and Israel, to name a few. Admittedly, there were still way too many nations that never shared in our glorious quarter-century as they were stuck in the old ways of state-run economies. The images of Iran, North Korea, Zimbabwe and Cuba come to mind.

But with all these successes and seemingly unlimited prosperity came complacency, greed and jealousy. People seem to have forgotten what the world was like in the 1970s. They don't remember the inflation, high interest rates, high taxes, high unemployment, diminished wealth, and low self-esteem. And with their memory lapse, they have chosen to resort to the instrument of government to even the score with those who had been more successful than they. The politics of class warfare and the economics of redistribution once again have captured center stage and are being employed as weapons to transfer power to the state.

The response to the crisis has been a complete repudiation of the supply-side Thatcher/Reagan brand of economics that brought with it such incredible prosperity. In its place, our country is left with stimulus packages based purely upon Keynesian economics and multi-billion pound bailouts of financial firms such as Bear Stearns and AIG. Congress has effectively nationalized the mortgage industry, much of the banking and auto industries, and is poised to do the same for the health care industry. It truly is unlike anything we have seen since the 1970s. George Orwell's nightmare is coming true.

Government spending as a share of total output has risen to wartime levels and the national debt is what Bill Safire of the New York Times used to refer to as a MEGO number, where MEGO stands for "my eyes glaze over." And our official national debt numbers don't include huge increases in the unfunded liabilities of federal government programs such as Medicare, Medicaid, Social Security, Civil Service Retirement and Health Care, Military Retirement and Health Care, Pension Benefit Guarantee Corporation, and soon to be U.S. National Health Care. And this doesn't even include the unfunded liabilities of all the state and local governments. Maybe these modern day Merlins have discovered the tooth fairy or Father Christmas, but I wouldn't bet on it. Who ever heard of a poor man spending himself into prosperity? Not I.

Already tax rates are scheduled to increase on January 1st, 2011, but that will only be the beginning. With this year's deficit of $1.4 trillion and the existing national debt, it's hard not to imagine enormous additional tax increases just around the corner. And, if taxes on people who work are increased and government payments to people who don't work are raised, don't be surprised if the number of people not working increases. And if these fiscal monstrosities weren't enough, President Obama is aggressively pushing his health care reform and energy bills through Congress.

On the trade front, protectionism is becoming increasingly "de 'rigeur" in the United States. Undeterred by logic or experience, the United States is venturing further and further into the swamps of a trade war with anyone and everyone who supplies our country with high quality products at low cost. Tariffs, quotas and countervailing duties are popping up everywhere. The Obama administration believes that imports cost Americans jobs as opposed to the correct answer which is that imports provide foreigners with the income to buy U.S. exports.

President Obama had made his distaste for NAFTA and the Columbian Free Trade Agreement clear in the 2008 presidential race and has now imposed duties on a number of products coming from China and has stopped Mexican trucks from entering the United States. In his stimulus package are old time protectionist "Buy American" provisions. For my part, I've always thought that producers were there to serve consumers, not the reverse. In cliché form, "the buyer is always right" and other such phrases touched the core of truth. And in an international context, my question to protectionists is if you found a store that sold high quality products at low cost, is your first thought "how can I boycott that store?" I don't think so.

When it comes to monetary policy, phrases such as "as good as gold" or "as sound as a dollar" appear to have disappeared from our lexicon. Over the past twelve months, the Federal Reserve has been printing money as if there were no tomorrow. Government always has a reason why it has to resort to the printing press, but the consequences are invariably higher inflation, a weaker currency, and higher interest rates. And so it will be this time as well.

Incomes policies are also going the wrong way on a one-way street. As conceived by us economists, incomes policies include all government economic policies that aren't part of fiscal, monetary, or trade policies. Basically, incomes policies comprise all the indirect ways government can affect business and the economy. These include regulations, restrictions, requirements, minimum wage, wage and price controls, health care, trade union activities, restraints on trade, and the like.

The prospects for prosperity appear bleak indeed as a result of new government incomes policies. The Obama administration is unabashedly pro-union and anti-business and has been pushing legislation on something called "Card Check", whereby unions can organize labor in non-unionized companies by requiring individual union members' votes be made public for all to see. This makes union retribution extremely difficult to avoid. Union members and prospective members won't be allowed the basic right of a secret ballot—pretty shocking.

In the United States the minimum legal wage companies are allowed to pay was raised by $2.10 an hour over the past two and one half years. As one might expect, the most vulnerable of our citizens are the ones truly hurt by such a policy, as they are in effect priced out of a job. While the increase in the minimum wage was passed and signed into law by the Bush administration, it has the full backing of the current administration. President Obama and the Democratic Congress are also pushing health care reform and cap and trade legislation, all of which would create a massive regulatory burden and increase taxes on U.S. firms and citizens dramatically. Additionally, government has stepped in with increasing calls for regulation of financial firms and caps on executives' salaries. None of these is a positive for prosperity.

So given the policy outlook in the United States, you should now understand why I am worried about our economy—all of the policy dials are tilted away from pro-growth economics. As a sign for hope, let me just add two points. First, while it is true that the United States has taken a big move to the left, what has happened is typical of the political pendulum. We have seen swings like this before, and the pendulum has always swung back again to pro-growth, good economics. And secondly, even though these policy changes are extreme, they can be undone as quickly as they were done. Nationalized companies can be privatized, increased tax rates can be lowered, and excessive spending can be cut. Our country is extremely resilient and has withstood lots of hardship and deprivation and bounced back better than ever.

In times like these the key is staying alive. Don't tell me about the return on my capital, I'm most interested in the return *of* my capital. It is imperative to stay informed so that you can successfully navigate today's treacherous investment climate.

And Daniel Frishberg can help you do just that. He has an uncanny ability to sense inflection points in the market, and in the pages that follow he lays out much of his view on what makes markets move. I've come to know Daniel and his wife Elisea very well over these past few years. So before you jump in, let me tell you a little bit of what I know about Dan Frishberg. I'll start by going all the way back to Daniel's routes in America.

Dan's grandfathers (maternal and paternal) came over from Russia at the beginning of the 20th century, generally to avoid the draft, which would have placed them both in the midst of the Czar's Army to fight the Russian Revolution. By the time Dan's maternal grandparents landed in America, there were restrictions already being placed on the immigrants who were coming to the United States to find jobs.

Dan's paternal grandfather became an author and educator. He refers to his grandfather as a pretty smart guy. Perhaps this was because Dan was somewhat the apple of his grandfather's eye. He took a particular interest in young Daniel, and allowed Dan to share in his own interest in 'the grand American lifestyle' which he believed was centered (and in fact had its roots) at the corner of Broad and Wall Street in New York. Before he was ten years old, Dan was tagging along with Grandpa down to the Stock Exchange. Much of what he does in his business and in his life today comes from the teachings of his grandfather in those early and very impressionable years of his life.

Continuing to frequent the exchange throughout his youth, Dan became familiar with the advantage held by the "specialists" in the exchangewhat we now call the "market makers" on the NASDAQ. At that level on the floor, you get to see the order flow. An ordinary investor or layman gets to see the transaction price. But the specialist not only sees the transactions, he sees the potential transactions . . . he sees the order flow. He knows if there are five buyers for every seller or vise-versa. He can see where the power is, and he's at great advantage to make money. Dan recognized this advantage, and still uses that knowledge today in his daily business of money management and investing.

After graduating from high school at the age of 16, Dan looked to the Marine Corps for his next bit of "real life education". His mom felt he could use some strong direction too, and signed the necessary documents for him to join up. He went to Okinawa and later he spent time on a carrier patrolling the South Pacific, and eventually he and a goodly number of his fellow Marines headed for Viet Nam. He was due to get out in 1965, and thanks to an acceptance for entry into Rockland Community College in New York, his military extension and near-return to Viet Nam was thwarted.

The commute from his home to college was about two hours each way every day in his mom's old Chevrolet, and that, plus classes, left little time for a social life. The payoff was that he became one of the top students in the New York Community College system, and New York University found him and offered him a full and free scholarship to attend.

After college, Dan held jobs in advertising, homebuilding, and health care, but all the while he actively followed and participated in the markets. At the age of 40, Daniel met his future wife, Elisea, who challenged him to put his skills to full use and share them with others. She saw that he was bright, articulate, and energetic. As for Elisea, she'd grown up in the Philippines and had not seen electricity until the age of 17. To say the least, they'd come from two different worlds.

And so, this 25 year old girl from the Philippines was the catalyst for the thought process that was then instilled in Dan Frishberg. He decided he'd begin sharing what he knew how to do with other people. At some point they were riding along in the car and Dan was complaining about something he'd just heard on the radio and how it didn't sound very smart to him. Elisea suggested he go on the radio himself, and do a better job. His first reaction was, "I don't know anything about being on the radio . . . but who knows? Maybe someday."

It wasn't long before Dan ended up back in the financial business. He went to work at Prudential Securities. Having learned the most interesting part of the money business on Wall Street, Dan was now learning what he felt was the most mundane part. But that little bit of conversation in the car that day about radio apparently sparked Dan somehow, because he ultimately ended up on the radio, doing a talk show (about money) in San Antonio. It was pretty much a first for the industry . . . there weren't a lot of financial shows on the air yet.

Since then the radio program has grown, as has the money management business Dan started on the side. This is where Dan began to see real opportunity. First, to grow his radio concept into something the likes of which had not been seen before. People who knew nothing about Wall Street didn't realize that they were learning about it, all the while being entertained by the people presenting the information to them. Ask Dan Frishberg what he's doing these days and he'll answer without hesitation, "I'm having the time of my life."

—**Dr. Arthur Laffer**

Acknowledgments

Dr. Arthur Laffer my mentor, teacher, and friend. You inspire me, and from you I learned what true greatness looks like. From you I gained the confidence to play in the big leagues. What you do is so unique, but you make it look so easy.

For your courage, your insight, your wisdom, and your singular contribution to the world, I am proud to call you my friend.

Sal Monistere.

For 20 years, you have dedicated a big part of your life to interpreting my thoughts and insights into Earth language. With your singular talent for communication in just about every medium, your ability to find an entertaining way to communicate any thought or idea, to bring order to chaos. I would hate to try to tell my story without you.

Prelude

My name is Sal Monistere. I came from radio. That's how I met Dan Frishberg, by the way; we bumped into each other in the hallway at a radio station about 15 years ago, and I've worked with him ever since. One day not long ago, he asked if I'd like to help him with a book project. Well, as his creative director, chief writer, editor, show announcer, and general producer for the past 15 years or so, I said, "Sure."

To be truthful, I don't think I've ever seen a book with a producer credit, but here I am. I've always told Dan that I thought the producer was the guy who would look at a performance, rub his chin knowingly, and say, "Well, what do you think?" At which point the associate producer would turn to him, rub his own chin (also knowingly), and say, "Gee, I don't know. What do *you* think?" In other words friends, this is Dan's book, and this is Dan's world—I'm just glad to be a part of it. And so as the producer, I only asked him if I could have a page or so here at the beginning because I want to make sure you're prepared for this.

I know. You're serious about this investing thing. And as a serious investor, you certainly don't have time to invest in a long barrage of verbiage from the guy who works behind the scenes. You're anxious to get to the part about the money. Fine. Just allow me if you will the minute or so it takes you to read the remainder of this little interjection before you get to the *real* beginning of the book. Because it's really, really important. And after that, I promise, no more delays.

Here's what we're going to do. The following is a rough transcription of Dan Frishberg's radio program; it was randomly selected and aired on April 8, 2009. It's combined with some of his personal notes for the show on that date. I just thought it would be good to include it here as an example of his work to prepare you for what you're about to discover in this book. You're about to discover the dynamics of Daniel Frishberg.

If you listen regularly (and adhere to his creed), you're probably reading this as you sit on a tranquil beach in some tropical haven, or are otherwise similarly enjoying the fruits of your investments. If on the other hand you've never heard his program, if you've never read his publications, you better hold on to your hat.

And one final note: Sometimes just looking over these scripts from Dan's shows can teach you an awful lot. We archive them all of course, so I've sort of sprinkled in a few more of them throughout the course of the book. Watch for them as they illustrate Dan's thinking and conversations with some real financial gurus.

OK, then, everybody ready? Fine, then cue Dan. Cue the intro music, and hit it—in three, two, one. . . . .

Studio Light On: On the Air (*Quiet Please*)

Sal: (*Show Opening.*)   "There's a billionaire locked inside you. The key to freedom is information, the kind of information you get right here on *The MoneyMan Report.* Here's Dan Frishberg!"

Dan: Good afternoon, *The MoneyMan Report* is on the air. Last time we talked I told you not to give up profits. Put tight stops on everything. (*We know the audience is dying to hold on to assets they bought a year ago, until they get even.*) Folks, this is suicide. The only thing that matters is the rally since March 9th. The rest of the equity is lost. It can only be retrieved through expert management, not patience, because there is nothing going on to suggest that the U.S. stock market will appreciate over the next several years. (*Don't forget notes from Closing Bell.*)

You don't hesitate about whether you should stop at a stop sign—a mistake can mean a huge collision. You have to always assume a Mack truck is barreling through. (*You just stopped at 100 of them and nobody was coming, but you still have to stop at the next one.*)

The people who are trying to tell you whether the current correction is real are the ones who didn't see the recession coming. Last year they told you the market was the buying opportunity of a lifetime, and the Fed and the U.S. Treasury didn't see it coming, either.

The only accurate strategic stock market decisions I see come from us. (*Credit here—our chief trader Karl Eggerss.*) How do we know so much? We do a MARKET X-RAY to measure underlying willingness to assume risk, or eagerness to reduce risk. And right now there's not enough information to tell us how deep the current pullback will be.

In other words, nobody knows how severe the current pullback will be, and the only choice is to treat it as though it'll be severe. You don't have to take losses because you're afraid to miss the upside later. When prices reach a point where they are too compelling to pass up, buyers will enter, and you can enter with them. Right now you don't have to know where that will be. Our research indicates that in the first few days of a rally the leading sectors are most likely to lead throughout that run. This time around it was China, base metals, consumer technology, platinum, and agribusiness. (*Add individual stocks below.*)

We understand enough to know that the stock market—on a risk-adjusted basis—is not the best use for your savings and does not deserve your loyalty. (*Analogy: You spend 20 years going in a straight line.*) They convince you that you don't need a steering wheel or brakes. Remember, you only have to get killed once to be a permanent loser! This is what happened to millions of people in our audience.

You've been taught to confuse saving with investing, and that's not right. (*Analogy: Saving is riding a train. Investing is flying a plane.*)

Investing takes skill and timing and economics; saving only takes repetition. Repetition is easy, it's done with memory cells. Investing requires brain cells and takes much more energy. (*Fewer people are good at it.*)

The fact is, you can excel at both flying and investing, but not if you don't stay awake, not if you don't learn how to steer *and land*. Landing is like selling your stocks. And not knowing how to land is what kills you.

(*Current short-term stock tip—just like last week: tight stops and sell decliners quickly.*) Don't be a hero and don't be a fortune teller. Remember this: You'll never find a 90-year-old who says, "I wish I had been more impatient." They generally say, "I wish I had been more patient, spent more time with my kids, and used dental floss."

(*For traditional long-term investors*): You are out of step with our times, but if you want something you can hang on to for a long time, consider the following:

TIPS, now bargain priced for 1.2 percent inflation. At some point, inflation will turn out to be much higher. The danger lies in government fudging the CPI numbers. In my humble opinion, this is a real danger, given the current administration. Even so, the fudging will come after the first signs of inflation. At these first signs of manipulation, TIPS should be sold.

(*If you're prepared to gamble long term and live with volatility . . . wait for the current correction to subside, then . . .*)

EJ/Ehouse—China: The Century 21 of China, connected to the very top of the Chinese government. They often take their commissions in shares of real estate projects. (*Great business with super prospects.*)

BIDU—the Google of China: What more do you have to say? They own 70 percent of the market versus 30 percent for Google.

The water business: Drinking water in bottles is already more expensive than oil. Americans will pay anything for it. Just tell them it's from France. Many of the richest countries are limited by their water supply. The world economy cannot grow without desalinization and other forms of processing, packaging, and transporting water. (*Make point that no replacement will be developed.*)

CGW is ETF, and there are also others: If you want to speculate, GE—may not be able to tolerate another leg down (*such as in 1930*), but otherwise a wonderful speculation. GE is a great company leading in everything that matters to human beings, currently facing uncertainty because of GE Capital.

(*Segment close.*)

(*Break*) . . . *The MoneyMan Report*—be right back with more—I'm Dan Frishberg, etc, etc."

(*Add copyright bug and standard disclaimer.*)

(*Cut to commercial, traffic, and weather forecast.*)

—**Sal Monistere**

Introduction: My Mission

Your life as an investor is about to change forever. Let me correct that, it's already changed. Your life as an investor, as a businessman or woman, your life as a member of the human race has changed in countless ways. And the changes are far more significant than the changes that came with the bicycle, the automobile, radio, and TV. In fact, the changes in your life from an economic standpoint are more profound than anything that's happened to the human race in 500 years!

Before the printing press only a select few could read and benefit from the developing information, the skills, the insights, and the opportunities that were sweeping the globe. The printing press allowed the transmission of radical new ideas in the fields of science, geography, and agriculture. Suddenly kings, queens, and nobles like Isabella, Elizabeth, Sir Walter Raleigh, and Columbus were becoming richer than anyone who had come before them.

World trade developed as these fortunate few figured out that we live on a spherical planet that circles the sun. They prospered far beyond their wildest dreams, sending ships around the world and conquering continents. They brought back tobacco, rubber, spices, tea, and gunpowder and sold it to their countrymen. They used the inventions of our Western civilization—information flow, transportation, science, and the art of modern warfare—to subdue the existing empires in all corners of the globe. In the process, they were able to accumulate most of the world's wealth, all for the benefit of that small European enclave that was the precursor of our civilization.

The seed of that revolution was planted with the development of the printing press, and it grew and developed for the next 500-odd years, culminating in the United States of America and the republic for which it stands. Since then, we've ruled the world. We've cured disease, shared ideas, and broadcasted drama, both real and imagined. We developed music, pictures, and sounds through motion pictures—then radio, then TV. We travelled to all corners of the Earth, to the moon, and then sent rockets around our solar system and our galaxy. And as the human race advanced through the transmission of our culture, we Americans—the beneficiaries of all this progress—became ever richer and ever more powerful.

It was easy to believe we'd developed an everlasting monopoly. Think of it. We owned every new idea and every new invention. We won every war, dictated policy, and defeated all comers in every competition. We created the best universities and research facilities. We accumulated almost all the wealth, power, status, and all the comfort.

We'd built a better mousetrap, and they came. The very best and the very brightest came to the United States to study and to invent. And they stayed, building the most prosperous country that could ever have been conceived in this little corner of the galaxy. To be sure, we put giant telescopes into orbit and learned to unravel the secrets of our universe going back billions of years. Can you conceive of just how long a couple of billion years is? It's the age of our planetary development, yet humans only learned to cultivate wheat 10,000 years ago. What a ride it's been as we developed communities, towns, cities, countries, and eventually alliances like Axis and NATO. So what now? What's changed?

If you haven't noticed, the worldwide web is ushering in a new order. Everyone on the planet can now easily acquire the same information and the same education. In past centuries, only that tiny group of nobles could collaborate in ways now made possible for the entire world, all due to the new technologies. But now, inspired by our freedom, ingenuity, courage, and inventiveness, the rest of the world has learned our lessons. They've duplicated our cultural advances. And they're catching up.

To many of us it feels as though we're falling back, but we're not; they're simply moving ahead at electronic speed. Life in this new century is all about new fuels, new power, new forms of energy and automation. All over the world, people are now having and doing everything our most creative ancestors dreamed of over the last 10,000 years.

What's changed you ask? Look around you. Today, you—along with six billion other human beings—woke up in a world without economic borders. We now know there are few limits on what our species can accomplish. We're taller and stronger; we run faster and live longer. And we enjoy comforts that even the nobility of the past could only dream of.

Today the borders are dissolving. There's no meaningful U.S. economy, no meaningful U.S. stock market. You're not limited to dollars, because you have access to every currency and every opportunity. You have access to six billion new customers, too, but you face fierce competition from six billion relentless competitors. You may find the idea frightening or daunting, but you can't afford to pretend it's not happening or you'll quickly be left behind. Billions of people are ready to sacrifice more and work harder than you are, because they're determined to give their families what you have.

But wait. We also have unprecedented advantages. We've been saving and accumulating surplus wealth for the past hundred years, while those new guys were still in the fields planting rice. They need our capital, and they're willing to pay premium prices for the opportunity to use it. We know exactly what they need and what they'll buy, and we've already been through all the steps they're about to take.

We can use our insights, our position, and our capital to finance the world's march forward, and allow those billions to work for us! We can help them win their battles and we can ride on their waves of success. Unfortunately, many of our fellow countrymen will opt instead to live in fear and denial. They'll hang on by their fingernails and squander their energy trying to hold the rest of the world back, to stifle the relentless advance of the human race as it catches up with us.

My mission for the 20-odd years left of my life is to help you use your capital efficiently and skillfully. To help put Investor 1.0 to rest and facilitate the birth and development of Investor 2.0—a new breed of investor, conscious and awake, who gets to take advantage of every new development and lead the human race to where it's headed anyway.

The best stock pickers, the most brilliant economists and financial thinkers join me daily on radio and TV; I meet with them socially, and we share business ideas. It's a joy for me because I get to process the best information on the planet and pass it on to you as quickly and as thoroughly as I possibly can. This book has proven to be very satisfying to me in that endeavor.

Of course, we won't ever be able to identify every opportunity. We'll never know whether we're missing something somewhere; in fact, I always assume we are. But we continue to march forward, always making progress, always stronger, always richer, keeping each other awake, and using our precious capital to help the billions around the world get what they want and need.

Turn the page and join me and the thousands of others who are getting to ride on the success and progress of our world, a world of six billion opportunities, six billion competitors. From an economic standpoint, it's a new world. A world without borders.

1

America the Dominator

How the U.S. Became the Most Powerful Country on the Planet

In this chapter...

- So you got the book. Let's see what you get.
- Who were they? Why did they come in the first place?
- A change comes: We're getting old, and printing too much money!
- Robin Hood, Sherwood Forest, and the Sheriff of Nuttin' Doin'
- Let's review: They come, they learn, they leave.

What's First?

Throughout the course of this book, there will be times when I'll want to get very specific with you. We'll talk about various investment techniques, and those techniques are as valid today and tomorrow as they were yesterday. The investments themselves, however, well let's face it, to get this book to you in the winter of 2010, I have to finish it in the autumn of 2009. I'm giving you my best ideas and strategies, although by the time you read this, some of them may have succeeded, played out, or even failed.

That's OK, because I'm giving you these ideas as an example of how you should be *thinking*. Take them in that spirit, because my mission is to help you transform yourself into the new species of think-for-yourself investor you'll have to be in this world without economic borders.

Our world is connected, networked as never before. We send our thoughts to each other everywhere and anywhere via e-mail, video conference, and streaming audio. We collaborate across borders and entertain each other across borders; we even finance each other across borders.

That means the rest of the world is at our doorstep; so yes, we'll talk a lot about how you can take advantage of this new "globalized" economy. But, make no mistake about it: For all intents and purposes, it is *American* ingenuity that created the wealth our neighbors want so desperately to share in. And there are plenty of great American companies to invest in—companies that stand as strong as the Rock of Gibraltar, companies that will continue to stand, continue to grow, continue to be some of the best investments available to make you rich, and richer.

As I'm writing this, you and I still need and want and buy devices from Cisco Systems—devices and ideas that are bargains to us, and extremely profitable to Cisco. I have little doubt that I'll be buying and selling that stock for the rest of my life. I've come to understand the company and the pricing of its stock; I can feel when it's a bargain, and when the money has been made. You can do it, too. It only takes a little experience and practice. Play with it, and you'll get it, just as you learned to throw a football or play ping pong, to shoot pool or draw blueprints, or to sing or dance.

I'll also be watching (and buying and selling) the Blackstone Group. I'll talk about these companies and others in more detail later, but for now, just imagine how Blackstone can fit into your life. This is not only about you and me buying into China, or the rest of Asia, or the rest of the world. It's also about them buying into us—remember, it's a global concept here. Look, the Chinese Sovereign Fund, along with smart people everywhere, has invested billions into Blackstone, and Blackstone, with its experience and savvy, used that money to buy companies, take them private, then develop and sell them, usually for a huge profit. I'm sure I'll buy and sell Blackstone many times over the course of the rest of my life. Again, you can easily learn to do the same thing.

The point to be made here is that this is not just us and *them*. It's all of us; it's a network. A worldwide network to be sure, but hey, it takes a phone connection or a computer connection the same amount of time to go around the corner as it does to go around the globe.

As an American, you're privileged to belong to a culture made up of inventors and innovators, a vast group of people who have been able not only to survive, but to thrive on their spirit of adventure and a vast store of knowledge—all long, long before our neighbors around the world began to "catch on." The fact is they've come a long way toward catching up. But their doors, as well as ours, are all unlocked; the walls are down, the economic borders no longer exist. It is to that point that I've put this book together.

So then, are you ready? Good. Now let's see how we ever got into this terrific position in the first place.

Why America Has Always Dominated: Part One

This is going to be the era when we Americans, the inspiration to the whole world, get to watch the ascendance of everybody else. It's hard not to think of yourself in decline, when everybody else is catching up. The truth is if we keep ignoring the free spirit and willingness to take a chance and assume the risk of losing what got us to where we are, we *will* see some decline. Much of this book is about how to think globally and share in the good fortune of those around the world that we have inspired. More than that, it's about how you can join me in getting rich helping them get what we have—that which they are determined to get!

Great. But don't be fooled. The real long-term success of the United States is still ahead of us. At the moment we may be slowing our own development by focusing on how we split the pie, rather than how we grow the pie, but life in this great country is cyclical.

Our society has more freedom than any other on this planet, and when the government's policies don't work out, we are better able to change policies and governments than anyone else. That's exactly what will happen. So, for now, you and I will make lots of money acknowledging that foolish U.S. policies are going to set us back a little, and give others with courage and initiative a chance to catch up and even surpass us in certain areas for a while.

Through that whole medium-term plan, don't forget for one minute that the worst bet ever conceived on planet Earth has been a bet against American ingenuity, the American economy, and American power. History is littered with the limp bodies of those deceased, and the shells that remain of those still alive, who have made that bet against the United States—from Hitler and Tojo, to Khrushchev and Brezhnev, to Saddam and Kaddafi. I, for one, do not plan to join them.

There are major reasons for our success. Our advantages over other nations are so profound they're difficult to overcome. Sometimes they lead us to make mistakes rooted in overconfidence and hubris, but we've always recovered, and when the whole world gets used to selling America, I can assure you, I will be buying.

The best and the brightest came to America, because they saw the big magic "O"—opportunity. And what created that opportunity was the very nature of the place itself. The guys who landed here way back when, landed in one of the most fertile, well-developed places on the face of the planet. It's a well-designed place, with better resources and a better setup than anywhere else in the world. From sea to shining sea, we have good, arable land. Easy to grow stuff on, it's the largest piece of contiguous arable land in the entire world. The middle of the country is made up of prairie land that is perfect for crops; it didn't even need to be cleaned up before farming. And there's more very good farmland on the East Coast, the West Coast, and down South.

There's good, arable land elsewhere in the world, but it's mixed in with mountains and jungles and deserts. We've never been saddled with the enormous burden of having to focus all our energy on trying to feed a country full of hungry, undernourished people, because it's never been hard for us to get large tracts of land set up to feed our population. Most other nations spend all their time and energy just trying to get food.

The next reason is travel. How easy is this? There are a couple of mountain ranges a few thousand miles apart, but other than that, it's flat! We've easily built roads for horses, roads for stagecoaches and buggies, roads for cars and trucks. We've easily built railroads north, south, east, and west. To build roads in most other countries, you've got to blast through mountains, or dig your way through treacherous land, or clear your way through jungles, and so on. It's slow, tedious, and very expensive work. And I'm talking about everybody: Europe, Asia, South America, Africa, China, Russia, all of them. They have tiny little pieces of arable land mixed with very, very rough terrain, where it's extremely difficult to move people around.

Those other countries need gigantic armies, too. Because of the layout of the land, armies need to be stationed all over the place in every key populated area. We've survived throughout the ages with smaller armies because it's so easy to move them around. These things are all important because the more resources you have the more creative you can become. We had started writing music and developing the arts while many countries were still trying to figure out how to build roads. And don't even get me started on the rivers and waterways in this country. Not only is the land fertile, we've got rivers that traverse the country in every imaginable direction.

Now, Europe has a lot of rivers, but they all move in one direction—without connecting. Here, the rivers connect! And it's so incredibly easy to use that network of rivers to move everything around. It's made it easy to develop cities, easy to get food there, easy to get equipment to the farms *and* to the armies.

America is also blessed with this great jagged coastline, which makes for great ports. It's easy for us to bring in big ships. They can anchor in those deep water bays just offshore and load their goods. In many of them they can dock right at the port city, which means easy connections to the rivers and more easy *means of transporting* people and goods. How could this *not* have turned out to be the dominant force in our world? It's really a great place to live and develop a population of people. We accomplish very easily things that are, for other nations, a considerable challenge. And that's just the beginning.

Why America Has Always Dominated: Part Two

Because of the physical nature of the United States, as described earlier, it was relatively easy to develop this country. And because that in and of itself created opportunities, it lent itself to an immigration of very intelligent, inventive, and creative people. They were attracted by this wonderful, fertile environment. And once they got here, they began to innovate, which only caused the advantages and opportunities to increase. It's what would happen in the NFL if the best team got to pick first in the draft. Imagine what kind of a team they'd build in a very short time!

I want to give credit to my good friend Harry Dent for this next line of thinking, and I'm compelled to include it because it really helps define the makeup of the generations of people who carry this country ever forward. Harry called one of them the "Bob Hope generation," and it had a particular role to play. You see, the generation that preceded it was the Henry Ford generation. They were very innovative, building and discovering new things, new technologies, the assembly line, and all the great inventions that served as the building blocks for many of the things that we use today.

The Bob Hope generation fought World War II and made it safe to live here. And it was Harry Dent who pointed out that these generations alternate. One generation invents and innovates; the next distributes and takes the innovation to the masses. One generation built the assembly line for cars, the next created gigantic car companies. Then came the Baby Boomers, to start the innovation process all over again. It goes without saying that computers, along with an incredibly high-speed Internet, have been the greatest of those achievements and contributions. Next? Maybe it will be a generation that will have computers that work without IT guys. Eventually we'll have a generation of computers that work so well and are so easy to manage that we'll be choosing them by how well they go with our décor, as we do with lamps and telephones.

So here are all of these very smart, very innovative folks in a land where opportunities abound, and there's another new and exciting one waiting around every corner. They take advantage of every one of these opportunities and are now inventing new ways to do things; one in particular is augmenting the human brain: computer networking and wireless digital communication devices. Together these elements facilitate the transmission of information at a speed past generations could not have even imagined.

All this led us to accelerate the speed at which more new innovations could occur. Suddenly our scientists are able to map the gene, and they can go back 15 billion years and look at things through the use of space telescopes and computer modeling. They're no longer limited to the use of their own brains. Every American benefits from the fantastic new ways to communicate with each other. Just like the rivers found in this country allowed a faster means of delivering goods and messages, the rivers of communication now flow at a speed never conceived before.

As the resources increased and improved, naturally, more folks wanted to join in on the fun. The Baby Boomers were the first ones fortunate enough to reap the benefits of all of those improvements in communication and manufacturing and so forth. This was a large generation of people. There were a lot of them to be strong, bright, and innovative. So you can see how things grew exponentially.

I guess the final word on this country's ability to dominate is this: Many of those other countries and their societies, particularly the Europeans, are traditionally noblemen with deep heritages. They're steeped in their owned strata, and they're basically stuck there. The folks who came over to America, however, were adventurous, ambitious middle-class people. They were merchants who were traveling, trying to develop more trade. Kings and queens and barons and baronesses don't care much about getting out there and developing trade. I guess they're too busy looking at their art. The merchants I spoke of (the middle-class folks) weren't so steeped in their traditions. They were far too busy, out there looking for new and exciting ways to conquer new frontiers and always seeking new adventures. You might say they were the artists, not the art collectors.

Why Things Are Changing

That's a lot of great news. Too good to continue this way forever? Well, let me say this: This generation I've been talking about, these energetic innovators, are, well, frankly they're getting old. And older folks don't have much mental flexibility. They don't particularly like to learn new languages; they don't care for political change. They don't even like to move (or be moved) around much. And once the key to progress becomes technology (instead of rivers), the transfer of knowledge can go anywhere. Like, for instance, to China.

Now, *there's* a place with little arable land, poor roads, and few rivers. So, why all the fuss about China? We Americans have so transformed the world that the new highway of knowledge is the Internet, and China and the rest of the world are using that technology to beat us at our own game. Rich and mature, many of us have a tendency to sit around thinking that we have all the advantages and no one could possibly have a shot at catching up with us. We forget that as we have prospered, we've taught them the game so well that they might become better at the game than we are. Our realization of this fact has been very slow in coming, but it will become clear quickly and suddenly. This book is not about fighting the inevitable; it is about loving it, embracing it, and riding that wave.

The problem for the average wealth of Americans in the near term is the fact that Americans just don't seem to get it. We're not getting the fact that when you print $12 trillion (that's what we're doing, you know) you weaken yourself. Other people in the world are beginning to compete. If we don't get it that you can't make laws dictating that folks buy cars they don't like (made by guys making $65 bucks an hour), then those folks are going to go out and buy cars that are made elsewhere. We don't seem to understand that when people get fed up and feel too much pressure, they can just up and move their businesses elsewhere.

We also don't seem to get it that you can't reward people for being lazy and slothful, and get the same level of ingenuity and aggression we've become used to over the last couple of hundred years. You can't punish people for being risk takers, because those people are going to either stop being innovative risk takers and/or they're going to go somewhere else and conduct business. We (and I say that collectively) don't seem to understand this stuff. How did we get to this point? How did this all happen? Let me see if I can explain it to you.

The people running just about all of the countries in the world have all been educated in the same places. They've all been attending our Ivy League schools, or Stanford or NYU or USC or the University of Chicago. The Chinese, the Pakistanis, the Japanese—the people running all of the countries around the world—were educated in the same universities in America as were many of our own leaders.

Here's the difference. The people running those countries majored in economics and finance. The people running our country studied political science and law. That's the reason they get it and we don't. That may be a bit metaphorical, and a bit oversimplified, but the bottom line is that's why they get it and we don't. There are other reasons, too.

Take for instance the idea that there have always been communists and socialists—and by the way, the idea of communism is not evil. The idea basically says, "Look, let's make things equal and spread the wealth, and make things fair for everybody." The only reason that idea has been fading, instead of growing and proliferating, is because it hasn't really worked that well.

You've seen it; these guys get into power and make bad decisions and then typically become selfish and corrupt. The idea of spreading the wealth, in and of itself, isn't a bad idea, it just doesn't work. The places where there have been incentives have generally become more productive, that's all.

Look, it's a nice idea. It would be lovely if we could all share and everybody could be equal and happy. My good friend and partner Arthur Laffer has a great story, and I've told it often and sometimes forget to give him credit, so this is Arthur's take on a classic tale, ok? It's the one about Robin Hood and his band of merry men. It's a wonderful, romantic story.

Robin Hood is in Sherwood Forest, he's got his green tights on, he's taking from the rich and giving everything to the poor; it's lovely, and he's a lovely guy. He gets the girl, Maid Marian, and it's terrific. And that's what some of our politicians would love to do. (No, not get the girl, that's another story.) They want to spread the wealth. Just like Robin. But there's a problem: How many times do you think those rich noblemen will keep going back through Sherwood Forest once they know Robin Hood is out there? See, that's the problem with this whole story. They rich guys stop coming! They've wised up to being robbed every time they go into Sherwood, so they quit going there!

The point is you can make the rules any way you want to, but if I have the ability through some technological advance to go anywhere I want to, I'm going. If I can use email or whatever to move my entire think-tank to Dubai in a split second, I'm out of here. But some of our politicians just don't get that. They don't get the idea that I've discovered that Robin Hood is laying in wait for me in Sherwood Forest, and so I have wisely found another route. What I don't get is that they don't get it.

Here's another contributing factor that is equally dramatic: a 24-hour cycle of cable TV, non-stop news and information. I participate in it, I love being a part of it, and if it's up to me, I'll never stop being part of it.

The people who run the media have figured out how to make it really interesting and entertaining. They've got beautiful people in beautiful make-up with beautiful smiles and great clothes. So now, you've got millions and millions of people all over the world watching 24-hour news. And it's not just the super-intelligent; everybody is watching, because like I said it's all so entertaining. So look what's happened here in the United States.

This past election is the first time—the first time in *history*—that an election has been determined by people who understand block voting, they understand the primaries, they understand everything about the election and the voting and the counting processes; they even understand the red states and the blue states, because they've studied the processes over and over. They've seen it presented like some sporting event on TV, but guess what? They never studied the history of western civilization, they never studied economics, they never studied literature, and they don't know what they were voting for, or who they were voting for, or what he or she stands for.

What's worse, they don't understand the impact of the things that they've said yes to—things that have been tried, but don't work. They don't know this stuff. They think they're going to be able to tax these rich guys, they think they're going to be able to force people to buy union-made cars from Detroit; they think all these things will happen, but they won't. And the reason, as my friend Arthur Laffer so eloquently stated when he gave me his spin on the story of Robin Hood, is that these folks will simply go somewhere else, where life (and doing business) is just not so hard or expensive.

So Let's Review

Indeed, America won the lottery when it came to being the ideal place to create an ideal land of milk and honey. Everything came together. The best and brightest came here. Individualism flourished. There were plenty of resources, plenty of space. We built our roads and railroads, and the Bob Hope generation liberated the world, first by winning World War II and then by mass producing some of the greatest innovations created by the human race. Our baby boom generation followed by inventing a whole new technology. Technology helped augment the human brain and solve virtually all of our problems, or so it seemed.

We now know that resources in the ground are fixed—either you have them or you don't. But with the aid of technology, *ideas* can now be duplicated anywhere. Inventiveness can spread anywhere. People used to come to the United States and learn, and then stay here and build their lives. Now they come here and learn, then go back home to do their inventing and innovating.

As a nation, we're less inventive, less adventurous, and as a nation where the predominant generation is pushing 60, we're less militaristic. We prefer a defense to an offense. And generally speaking, most folks in this country are not as hungry as we as a nation once were. By nature of the fact that you're reading this book, I can only surmise that you're working toward excluding yourself from that group. Well done, Investor 2.0.

So, how do we do this? We emerge from the fog of denial that has us trying to replay the 1990s. We stop feeling threatened by innovative, smart, hard-working people around the world who are determined to work harder than we do. We use our capital to develop natural resources to feed their growth, as a couple of billion of them move from the country to the city, following *our* model to build their countries.

The success of technology companies in the 1990s attracted so much capital and created so much capacity in those areas that profits were cut and monopolies were lost, thereby making those very areas less fruitful for investors. Some of those businesses will be fine, but to get my investment dollar today, a company must have a brilliant Asia strategy, no matter where in the world it resides.

You and I will be able to make big money, easily and without that much creativity, by financing the finding, processing, storing and transporting of the building blocks of society—the things you absolutely have to have to move billions of people from the country to the city. Those billions of determined American-lifestyle *wannabees* will need every bit of copper, zinc, cement, platinum, titanium, iron, steel, coal, oil, and pure drinking water that they can lay their hands on, and we've got the resources to help supply them. These kinds of investments are now easy to make with exchange traded funds, structured notes, and bonds. I'll be naming many of the ones I'm committing my money to, and I'll explain strategies you may have never seen or heard before. They're strategies the very rich have had access to for a long time.

You've always had access to everything you'll learn in this book; I've simply compiled it for you, which will at the very least save you a trip to the library. Face it, nobody goes to the library anymore (and we'll talk about that a little later). At any rate, armed with this information, using your capital to finance this most powerful and unstoppable movement in the history of the human race should be a no-brainer. How could you *not* want to own a company that provides inexpensive online education to the Chinese to teach them English, technology skills, and whatever else they need to know to bring hundreds of millions of them into the middle class? How could you not want a piece of a government-owned real estate broker in a country that's preparing to move a group of people equal to the entire population of the United States into new cities? How could you *not*?

We've had some building booms in the United States, and many of us have made some pretty good money participating in them. But close your eyes and consider this: In the next 10 years, the Chinese are going to build—from the ground up—the equivalent of New York City, Los Angeles, Chicago, Atlanta, Miami, Phoenix, Houston, Dallas, Fort Worth, Denver, and San Francisco. Where in the world are we—the *cross-border* citizens of this economically borderless planet—ever going to find, mine, and produce enough raw materials to do all that? How are we going to store it or transport it all?

I'll tell you: We are going to need a lot of help. The people in China are going to have to get labor and materials from Australia, Indonesia, South Korea, and Taiwan, as well as South America and Africa. Just think for a minute about how much capital Europeans and Americans used and how much wealth we created building out projects like that over a period of 200 years. And now, think how rich will be those who are instrumental in helping all this happen, when the development is compressed into just a couple of decades! Throughout this book I'm going to talk to you about how you and I are going to provide financing for all this.

As you're reading, keep this picture in your mind. Keep reminding yourself about how those of us who finance this largest social movement that has ever happened are going to make more money than anyone has ever made on this planet before. Think about how much money is going to be made just helping these hundreds of millions—no, these *billions*—of new middle-class citizens of our borderless world get pure drinking water. (You know, of course, that wars are already being fought over drinking water in Africa, and Americans already pay more for a liter of drinking water than they do for the same amount of gasoline! "Just tell them it's from France!" laugh the bottlers.)

You and I already know exactly what these billions of new middle-class citizens of our new borderless world are going to be buying, and we already know how to help them get what they're totally determined to get. There's no doubt they will succeed, so who wouldn't want to help them get there—and be paid very well for doing so?

Welcome to the New World, Investor 2.0

Now, here's an absolutely *crucial* admonition. I don't know anything about you. Some things that are great investments and projects for me may *not* be right for you. You may have special tax, personal, and other factors that I know nothing about. As *the* most up-to-date, smartest, *upgraded* investor—as Investor version 2.0—you must get into the habit of evaluating ideas instead of just finding people you can trust to lead you. I'll talk about that a lot in this book, but take this reminder seriously, right here and right now:

Think through the ideas I give you. Don't just go out and commit money to things I'm investing in without taking the responsibility of knowing *exactly* what you're doing. This book is to entertain you, and to condition your mind to take advantage of the huge opportunity that is now open to you. Take my work as a place to start the research to support your evolution into a whole new life form—a new species of investor—a conscious investor who is free of denial, and who actually invests for money instead of self-esteem.

At the very top of the food chain, right now, all the players know that power is synonymous with responsibility. I can promise you with absolute certainty that you will begin to attract great wealth (and not lose it) the minute you decide to be totally responsible for your every thought and action. My life, my happiness, and my wealth are not determined by President Obama, Goldman Sachs, The Fed, The Hedge Funds, The Chinese, or CNBC. You can be equally free, equally powerful, and you can start getting richer, right now.

From this moment forward, take responsibility for every single thing you decide to commit your money to. You have all the time and all the opportunities you could ever need. The very richest people in the world all know this:

> Your money belongs in YOUR pocket unless you have something compelling to commit to. The very rich don't feel pressure to hurry up and invest. They know the resource that is most scarce and in most demand is money. They have it, and everyone else needs it. That means they can be very choosy about where they commit.

You can do exactly the same; you can learn to think like a rich person in a world of infinite opportunity, a world without economic borders. And starting right now, today, you're well on your way. Now then, let's see what challenges you're facing.

Before the Borders Came Down

How the Wall Street Liars Shot Themselves
(and the Rest of Us) in the Foot

I n this chapter . . .

- Wall Street liars: They don't advise, they just sell you stuff (and take commissions).
- The liars shot themselves in the foot; Banks fail, brokerages now broker than ever.
- Gates opens Windows; Nanotechnologists will follow.
- Lemmings love velvet; Then, stay tuned for "The Cleavers"
- China creates their own stimulus package, but they'll need steel, and iron, and zinc . . .

Liar, Liar—Starts the Fire!

It wasn't too many years ago that I did a project called *Wall Street Lies*. It was a package of audio CDs that I put together because there was a story to be told. A lot of it was about the right and wrong of what was going on at the time with many of the brokerage firms, insurance companies, and other people who were selling financial products.

I want to rehash a bit of that story with you here, because the results of those activities directly relate to the recent failures in our financial system. The actual cause of our economic woes is better told in the title and subheads of this book. Indeed, the new competition brought about by today's lightning-fast communications are the essence of what we'll discuss in this book. I just think the selfishness of these Wall Street Willies finally caught up with them, and the results are evident in our headlines over the past couple of years. Indulge me for a few pages if you will.

Wall Street Lies was my means of pointing out the myths, the facts, and most importantly, the lies you'd hear every day. On TV, on the street, from your neighbors (most of whom didn't know any better), and in many cases from your "adviser."

One of the many things these guys would tell you is that, although what you do matters considerably, *when* you do it isn't really all that important. Most of them, then and now, would have you believe that timing the market is impossible anyway, so why lie awake at night trying to figure out how to do something that can't be done? "You can't time the market" remains one of the biggest of all the Wall Street lies.

If you've lost lots of money on good companies that have been successful, or will at least at times be successful, you already know what a foolish idea that is. The truth is you'd *better* time the markets. I for one am doing my best to seek good timing in everything I do during my remaining 8,000-odd days left on this planet.

Those so-called experts would also suggest that you rely on diversification to keep you safe. This means just invest in a little of everything, instead of choosing the place to use your financial power. I don't think that idea ever made sense, but when the entire market was on the rise and everything was going up together, it made a good story, and it justified assuming risk without knowing exactly what you were doing.

Presumably that also made it alright to rely on advice from people who didn't know much about investing. You probably don't need an exposé on that idea at this point, because so much money has recently been lost by good, intelligent people who were lulled into believing they were safe. They figured they were diversified and didn't have to be aware of the world changing around them.

But the world has changed gradually and imperceptibly each day. We reached a tipping point, and all the markers for carelessness, arrogance, hubris, excessive risk and insensitivity to timing came due at the same time. It was as if suddenly someone shouted "FIRE!" on a crowded planet and everyone in the world ran for the exits at the same time, catching most investors completely off guard—and doing away with decades of savings.

The irony is, all anyone ever wants to know, all the pundits on TV redundantly ask, all the callers want to know when they call in to the radio hosts is this: "When are we going to get back even? Is the economy going to be able to sustain recovery?"

These are precisely the *wrong* questions to be asking. Our economy may not *ever* be the same as it was. My guess is it will feel good for a while, as we digest the speed injected by the Fed and the Treasury, but although speed will certainly wake some people up and make many feel energetic and positive for a little while, it isn't real nourishment—and that good feeling just doesn't last.

The point is this: Who cares! Today you woke up in a world without economic borders. That world will grow at four, five, or even six percent for the foreseeable future. For the most part, the growth around the world will support real economic development in countries we never thought of back in the 1990s. Great American companies, smart American investors, and powerful American financial institutions will feed, finance, and help create the steady forward march of civilization around the world.

From my vantage point here in the autumn of 2009, I expect that by the time you read this book the United States will be temporarily enjoying a feel-good recovery. And the odds are very high that the country of Indonesia will be enjoying terrific economic improvement. Indonesia is country nobody around here even thinks about much. Let us discuss Indonesia.

Most of us still envision Indonesia as it was 10 years ago: violent, despotic, and corrupt. To the contrary, Indonesia has developed into one of the most democratic, free-economy Muslim countries in the world. It's true that their economy has been shaken and set back a couple of times, but Indonesia provides inexpensive labor and materials to China, and the Indonesian economy gets freer, healthier, and more robust every day.

China is developing a stronger civil court system and learning to protect property rights, but to me, it still carries some risk along those lines. The Indonesia Closed End Fund, (IF) is giving me a chance to invest in a fast-growing, free economy with a hugely profitable customer. For me, this is a much smarter and more rewarding way to use my capital to help people get what they want, compared to trying to transport myself back to the past.

Along these same lines, you should study up on the Taiwan Fund, another closed end fund. Taiwan and China are in the process of becoming friendlier. This could make Taiwan, right now, the single most profitable place on the planet to invest. Taiwan has always been a leader in producing high-tech products like computer chips, and the Taiwanese have huge investments throughout mainland China and all of the South Pacific. Investing in Taiwan not only allows investors to capitalize on Taiwan's dynamic economy, but it also allows investors to reap the growth and investment potential of mainland China and other emerging economies of the region.

By the way, "closed end" simply means these are funds that trade like stocks on U.S. exchanges, instead of being issued and redeemed every day by their promoters. This gives you another way to be smart. Sometimes these funds sell at a premium to the value of their assets, and sometimes they trade at a discount. When you buy a fund for less than the value of its assets, you can make money due simply to the market changes, in addition to whatever good things happen to the companies you're financing. You can check any number of free websites to tell you whether these funds are selling at a premium or a discount.

Rah, Rah, Rah! MatchBook U!—The Curriculum

I'd mentioned those times when there were a lot of lies being told by the brokerage firms, insurance companies, and other people who were selling financial products. I must say, they had some interesting sales techniques, but this was one of my favorite parts. They'd always include this old story about an investment formula. (And wouldn't it be nice if there actually *was* a simple formula?) It was especially designed for old people, and they teach it at Matchbook U. Now for those of you who've never heard of Matchbook U, it's that school that teaches the various correspondence courses seen advertised in magazines or on the back of matchbook covers—courses typically supported by big brokers and insurance companies. (It's where the "financial planners" went to school.)

But about this formula: it says that old people should take the number 100, subtract their age, and then the result is the percentage of their money that should be in stocks, and the rest should be in bonds. In other words, if a person is 80 years old, he should have 20 percent of his money in stocks and 80 percent of it in bonds; 50 years old, he should be half in stocks, half in bonds, and so on.

I'm convinced that this old formula was designed by 40-year-olds making $30,000 a year who have no idea of what old people need. Anytime I've encountered an 80-year-old and offered a suggestion about what they should buy, well, the really smart ones look at me and say, "I want to know what *you're* buying." I think the guys who design this type of plan think they're catering to an elderly person's concern about when they might die. I simply advise them that the real problems come if they continue to live! Usually we have a good chuckle over that point and then talk some good common sense. That's what old people really like anyway—good, common sense.

So these stockbrokers and these insurance salesmen—any of these guys who'd want to sell you some kind of financial product on behalf of some company or institution—they had come to refer to themselves as financial consultants, or planners, or advisers. I'll give you the real definition of those terms later, but implicit in these words is the idea that these guys are hired by you and paid by you, and that their responsibility is to do what's best for the guy paying them—and that of course would be *you*!

Nothing could be farther from the truth. An insurance guy is a selling agent, and he *doesn't* work for you. He works for the insurance company, which has a particular agenda: They want to sell their products. And your stockbroker? He's not a registered investment adviser. He's not obligated to act on behalf of you any more than a real estate broker is obligated to act on behalf of the buyer; on the contrary, he acts on behalf of the seller.

These MatchBook U graduates rarely have a clue about how to make money. They learn how to be your buddy. They learn (a) to convince you to put a lot of eggs in a lot of different baskets, and (b) to remember the names of all these various financial products. The final exam at best can only determine that they have good basic financial hygiene.

Don't misunderstand. I'm not saying your buddy is a bad guy. I'm saying that you may think he's going to be right there for you and that he knows how to make money. But there's no evidence of that; in fact in most cases he's probably not even making a lot of money himself. Go ahead. Look out in the driveway—what kind of car is he driving?

Listen, the important thing to know is that these guys went to some place that showed them how to magnify the need for insurance and front-end loaded products, and the story they tell you is the same one they tell all of their clients. They'd hand you a laundry list of financial products: "Here! Take a look at this list, and don't worry about whether it's a good time to buy because everybody knows there's no better time than the present. And since you don't have a clue about *what* to buy or when to sell this stuff anyway, well, heck, you might as well buy it all from me, right?"

And even if they loaded up on the fees and charges, if they only had the flexibility and good sense to come up with a new diversified portfolio of investments that provided the capital to fuel the inevitable development of the other side of the world, well then, they might actually *earn* their commissions and charges. But that would require them to change their strategy according to the opportunities at any given moment in *time,* you see? It would actually take *timing*. For these guys, that would be a whole new concept!

No wait, hold on, there's more—we're havin' fun now! Let me give you an example of how a typical financial planning meeting might go with one of these Matchbook U grads; maybe you've been through this one before. Let's say you're married, and you're the bread-winner for your family. Let's say 40 years old with two kids. So this guy comes out and takes the information on you and then feeds it into his computer. It comes back with a story about how much insurance you don't have and, of course, what you really *should* have.

So the computer says you need "this much" insurance because God forbid, if you were to die, your spouse would have "this much" of an income shortage. Note that his computer assumes that even though you're only 40 years old when you die, your spouse will do nothing but sit around and watch TV for the rest of his/her life—and be *totally* dependent on your life insurance policy. Did you ever think about that?

"And besides," he says, "your spouse isn't going to help people around the world get what they want. That nest egg you're trying to create is *not* going to help finance the greatest social movement in history." If you're listening to this guy, you're being duped my friend. You're being told that timing is unnecessary, and that appropriate action is not achievable. And the worst of it is that this kind of thinking causes you to commit huge amounts of your capital in the wrong place, and in fact it *assures* that your spouse is going to need a huge infusion of cash. It also assumes that once your lonely widow or widower gets that cash infusion, they'll continue to be totally ignorant of the greatest transformation in the history of the human race. I hope you get this. Otherwise, you're going to *need* all that insurance.

Hey, what if the computer assumes you'll only be disabled? Nope, sorry, the answer is still essentially the same. The assumption is that no matter what bad thing happens to you your family will just sit in front of the TV for the rest of their lives, and must be supported *without digging into the principal* of the insurance policy. In other words, as the breadwinner, you have to have enough insurance so that the income from the insurance pays for every expense the family incurs *ever again*, even if you die at age 40!

OK, I'll stop there. This book isn't about insurance anyway, right? What I'm addressing is the people who would come out and sell you a cornucopia of financial products using those silly arguments cited above, and posing as financial planners. Now that we've done that, I assume you realize that the insurance policy our 40-year-old friend almost bought wouldn't have been his best move. Let's talk about some alternatives. Let's talk about bonds.

One of the reasons people don't want to learn about bonds is that they seem a little boring. And in a way they are. You don't get that thrill of victory or the agony of defeat coming directly out of the investment. *You're investing with certainty instead of uncertainty*. I don't see anything particularly wrong with that. But people who are looking for an easy place to learn often don't like a situation where they might have to think. I can tell you I'm not really the right guy to try to sell bonds to. Actually, I'm the kind of guy who really needs them, but they just don't feel that appealing to me because I'm always looking for the big score. I'm an impulsive and greedy person; I like the big score.

In truth, I learned about the bond market as a necessity, and I learned about it very late in life, but the minute I did my life improved, my results picked up, and lo and behold I made more money in the stock market because of bonds. I'm absolutely positive that you too will do better in all of your investments—stocks, commodities, metals, real estate—all of it, if you understand bonds.

Did you know that the bond market is 10 times the size of the stock market? It has 10 times more money in it. The reason is because the very, very rich who control most of the money know that their money, as you'll hear me say throughout this book, belongs in their pocket. If you only get one thing, this needs to be it: *Your money belongs in your pocket*. The only reason for you to invest your money and take risks is because you have a real conviction that you're going to get back much more money than you put in. Otherwise you can put your money in a safe place (like a bond) where you know you're going to get paid back and get paid well for its use—especially in a scarce capital environment like we have right now. Our 40-year-old friend should hesitate on that insurance policy we talked about earlier. He ought to try to learn a little about bonds.

Good Ol' Matchbook U—The Faculty, Staff, and Graduates

Which takes us back to the subject of what that insurance salesman (and guys like him) have sold the American public. They've sold you a bill of goods that has, in the final analysis, cost them their own jobs. And in the course of explaining that, I might as well tell you why it's so hard to get information about bonds. I know it's hard because people are always asking me about how to do the research. *Is there a book? A CD, a video? What can I read? What is there to know? Is there a basic course somewhere? Why doesn't anybody teach you about bonds?* Well, this brings up the bigger question: How do you learn about *anything* financial these days?

Unfortunately, the answer is that most folks learn from their financial planners and their stockbrokers. All right then, who are these people anyway; are they experts? I'll let you be the judge, but let's analyze it. First of all, how do they get trained? Well, some go to real schools and get real finance degrees, but generally those guys end up working in a big building somewhere over in the investment-banking department doing the big money deals.

Now the salespeople—the stockbrokers you get to talk to—they don't usually have that kind of education. They're people who are more likely to have a bachelor's degree in, well, in *something*. Who knows, maybe finance, maybe economics, maybe accounting, whatever. And then they get sent to, that's right, good old Matchbook U. You know, the alma mater of those guys we just talked about a few pages back: The guys who graduate from those courses you see advertised on matchbook covers who then go on to be salespeople.

These stockbrokers and salespeople are, if not coerced, certainly *encouraged* to get that education. When you go to a financial planner it's with the idea of making more money, of having an improvement in your bottom line, but you see, these guys don't learn techniques to make more money; they only learn how to execute what we laughingly call *Modern Portfolio Theory*. It's what they believe to be the skill of engaging in an arbitrage strategy to allocate assets that garner a risk-free profit—a profit based on purposely choosing to have your actions relate to something other than the real world or to the times in which you live. More precisely, it's their *lack* of skill to engage in arbitrage.

What they're trying to accomplish with their *Modern Portfolio Theory* is to convince you that there's nothing to know and that timing doesn't help—that in fact, timing doesn't really matter at all. The theory these guys work on is getting you to buy a little bit of everything, presumably so that you can be a *little bit* wrong all the time.

Oh, and it's important that you understand this: these guys that you think of as brokers or salesmen are actually called "registered representatives" of a FINRA firm, of a brokerage firm or a broker-dealer. (A broker-dealer means that they are either the middleman in a transaction or they sell you stuff from their inventory, which would make them a dealer.) So the company is actually called a broker-dealer, and your salesman-guide-adviser is actually called a registered representative. What's funny—well, actually it's *not* funny—is that he or she is *not permitted to originate any advice.*

Don't misunderstand: Many of them will make it *seem* as though they are giving you advice. But let me say it again: They are *not permitted to give advice*; they're simply there to pass on the position of their firm. It involves quite a mess of bureaucratic technicalities, but it would probably help you to know the story of the SEC regulation of advisers versus what used to be the NASD (and is now called FINRA) and its regulation of broker-dealers and their registered representatives.

You see, a registered investment adviser is regulated by the SEC. He or she has an obligation to act in a fiduciary manner—that is, to act on behalf of and for the benefit of the client and give advice when he's acting in the capacity of an adviser. Yes, there are conflicts of interest, which are permissible, they simply have to be disclosed.

Now, a *broker* is the actual sales company. Generally speaking, they're representing *not the investor*, but the company that needs to raise the money. So they owe fair treatment, yes, but there's not a fiduciary responsibility to advise, and I'm talking in particular now of your registered representative or salesman. His obligation is to act *on behalf* of his broker-dealer, who is in the business of raising money for the company who wants *you* to invest in *them*. You need to understand that it's not possible to serve both masters, because what is defined as a good deal for the investor must then be a concession by the target company that the investor is investing in. Said another way, if it's a great deal for the company, then it's *not* such a great deal for the investor.

Imagine a conversation in which the broker-dealer goes to the big company, let's say IBM (or anybody really), and he says, "Well, interest rates are very low right now and there's a very big risk spread, so a company like yours, which is very well known and obviously solvent, is gonna be able to get a very low interest rate right now. And so I recommend that you go out and float a bond issue." Again, obviously, if it's good for the company trying to raise the money, it can't be good for the person who lends the money at a low interest rate. That makes sense, right?

Now, let me get back to the story about the advisory and its requirements to disclose. Some years back the brokerage firms found that a lot of people were concerned about conflicts of interest. This happened around the end of the '90s when it became obvious that there were tremendous conflicts of interest and the brokerage firms weren't handling them very fairly. People started to think (and say) that they would rather have an adviser who had a fiduciary responsibility to the investor, that they would be able to trust them better. (I think the public was right at that time.)

But the brokerage firms came up with the idea—and by the way Merrill Lynch was in the forefront of this—they added the word "adviser" to their name and created what they called wrap accounts, accounts which made them *look* like an adviser. So now they have a new name, and instead of paying them individual commissions per transaction, you'd pay them a fixed amount per year. Which, by the way, would typically add up to a little more than you'd otherwise pay in commissions.

So now the brokerage firm *looks* like a registered investment adviser. The difference being that the registered investment adviser owes that fiduciary responsibility because he receives *fees* for his advice. The brokerage firm makes *commissions* by raising money for the company that you invest in (rather than representing you, the investor). It's important that you understand that distinction.

Using the word "adviser" was deemed to be deceptive; it would make the brokerage firm look like a registered investment adviser and give the investor the *impression* that they're acting as his fiduciary. So the position of the brokerage firms' industry was that they should get a special dispensation to use the word "adviser," but under SEC rules, if you use the word adviser you must disclose any conflicts of interest. See, if you're a registered adviser, people are naturally trusting that you're their fiduciary. Moreover, the brokerage firms were not only seeking SEC permission to use the word adviser, but special dispensation to avoid disclosure of their conflicts of interest! I hope this gives you some insight into the relationship and the difference between the two. The easiest way to remember this is when you hear the word adviser beware. Whew.

Now then, where was I? Oh, yes, finally we've come to the heart of the matter, and here it is. Is the brokerage firm you're about to do business with a company of experts? Could you trust them even if they *wanted* to give you good advice? And what about that sales guy, the broker or registered representative, even if he really wants to give you good advice, is *he* an expert?

First, let's address the companies. You have to remember that now, as we look back on everything that's happened over the last 20 years, you can see that the scandal at the end of the '90s was all about the brokerage firms. Their analysts were actually out there touting stocks, and it later came to light that they were simultaneously sending e-mails literally laughing about some of the recommendations they'd made.

So they were obviously not following the advice that they were giving other people; they were making a mockery of their own business dealings. Here's where it gets interesting. Later, in fact just a few years ago, they actually began to follow their own trading advice. And when they did, they put themselves out of business in just one cycle! They're now owned by companies that had to get government money to bail them out because *they* followed their own advice too!

The biggest broker, the one that was in the forefront trying to use the word *advisor* without disclosing its conflict of interest, was actually bought by a bailed-out bank. Then, at the last minute, you remember the scandal; at the last minute, Bank of America wanted to back out, but the government forced the CEO to buy the brokerage firm. Which of course proceeded to pay itself huge bonuses with money that was earmarked for bailing out the business! Those, my friends, are the companies we're talking about.

Now how about the brokers themselves? They were trained by their brokerage firm, which understands all of the brokers' capabilities and training perfectly, right? We presume the company understands the abilities of the salesman or registered representative. They educated this guy, they understand his skill set; they're actually paying him money *because* of his purported expertise, right? Right? All right then, so let me ask this very simple question: How often do you think they ask him for advice about what *they* should do with *their* portfolio? How about their bond portfolio in particular? Now you have to ask yourself what it is that they want to sell *you*. And then ask yourself if this is the guy you want to buy *anything* from. Anything?

In the Headlines: Gates Opens Windows (Film at 11)

At one time, not long ago, the world relied on complicated, sequential, and difficult-to-learn language routines to give directions to their computers. Then Bill Gates and friends devoted their lives to coming up with an innovative way for people to use simple graphics to give orders to their computers. All the computer geeks in my life at the time told me that this invention Gates had come up with (Windows) was a waste of time. You just didn't need it, they told me. Gates and friends didn't listen. They were rewarded. They became some of the richest people in the world.

Ten years from now, the richest man or woman in the world will run a nanotechnology or genetic engineering company that doesn't yet exist, selling a product that hasn't yet been invented. But I can assure you that the company, and the inventions it brings to humanity, will be helping many people get something they really, really want. And I assure you it will be financed by the same stock market that has been keeping me happy, busy, and rich for a lifetime. And although the stock market is a good device for putting your capital to work helping people get what they want, it is certainly not the only one.

And Now, Stay Tuned For the Cleavers

Here's a simple story dramatizing how Investor 1.0 lives. It is a story of how the lead lemmings will drive headlong over a cliff, and the rest will follow. Bear in mind, the setting for this story could have just as easily occurred in the stock market, the bond market, the commodity market—you name it. I actually first wrote this for a radio monologue in 2000, when I heard the media saying that even though the Fed is pulling money out of the economy and tightening, the stock market was "still safe because tech companies don't have to borrow money anyway." Of course, in their feverish excitement, those experts forgot that if nobody is selling cars and tires and regular stuff, there wouldn't be anybody to buy all that software they were so excited about. Anyway, here's my little story, and just imagine if you actually heard this on the next Bloomberg update.

A family—let's call them "The Cleavers" from Southern California—gets caught in the rain on their way home with their new velvet painting of John F. Kennedy. The paint washes off and the painting is ruined, but under it is an original painting signed by George Washington! The Washington original is a painting of George's cat, and it isn't very good, but his signature alone is worth $400 million. So there's a run on velvet paintings. Every John F. Kennedy on velvet is getting snapped up. There isn't any velvet left to buy. People are traveling the country buying velvet paintings from each other. They're going for as much as $20,000 each, and the prices are rising! Most people aren't even going home to wash the paint off to see if there's another Washington under it. Most of them are just selling them to the next velveteer.

Now, families across the country are pulling their kids out of school so they can have more time to scour the country looking for velvet pictures—velvets of Elvis, JFK, even Dolly Parton velvets are rising in price! We see an interview of one smart family who got in early. They have a house full of velvet! They haven't really had time to wash the paint off them. "We don't have time . . . we're too busy traveling the country buying 'em up. Fortunately we had some money put away; it *was* earmarked for the kid's college fund, but, well, anyway, we're just gonna hold onto 'em without lookin' under the paint, because in the short time since we've been into it, they've gone from $1,000 to $20,000. By next year they could be at a million each and then, who knows? We'll just hold on to 'em; at this rate, we'd be stupid not to."

Now, Kmart has just released a story saying they're going to switch their stores over to 'all velvet, all the time' and stay open 24 hours. When asked if they plan to keep pace, Wal-Mart says, "No. We'll just concentrate on selling our regular merchandise. If people don't have clothes and food, we don't see how they can continue to keep searching for velvet paintings of Elvis."

Meanwhile, in a related story, Joe Granville's decided to get ahead of the market. He's putting together a syndicate to build a 200-story building. "It'll be the biggest building in the world," he proclaims. "We're going to put it in Shanghai! Four billion square feet! That's with a 'B,' baby! And here's a little news tip for ya: We're gonna produce velvet pictures of Hannah Montana!" OK, I think you get the gist of my story. You know, I've never really cared for those velvet paintings. I don't know; to me, they just look sort of, well, *cheap*. But maybe it's me.

Where would it end? The government and well-meaning regulators have now seized the right and the obligation to decide which prices are right and which ones are wrong. You won't have a right to be brave *or* stupid. Speculation is to be prevented, but speculation is what brought about the most productive research and innovation, and people who became rich by taking a chance on their beliefs.

You won't have room for Kohlberg, Kravis and Roberts, Warren Buffet, or any of the Internet research and development that now shapes our world. None of that would have happened without the feverish speculation.

You wouldn't have cable TV or Berkshire Hathaway without severe drops. No bargains, nobody gets rich, no room for people who are better or braver to do well. It's obvious that innovators, speculators, bargain hunters, as well as the brave and the smart, the overconfident and the dumb, will have to go elsewhere. In past generations the United States was the place for them to go.

Now that we aren't allowed to do that in the United States, the best and the brightest, along with the dumb and the overconfident—two sides of the same coin—will go elsewhere.

This brings up the basic truth that one of my most important mentors pointed out to me in the Marines during wartime 40 years ago. Courage and insensitivity are the same behavior. Only the situation determines which one you are practicing, and they both feel the same. You have courage? You're going to have to learn to compete in a world of six billion people, because most of the profit is going to be made somewhere else, outside the United States, maybe for quite a while.

Everything 'Made in China'?
So Sorry, Not Soooooo . . .

Now let's see, oh wait, look! A 25 percent drop in the price of Mosaic stock, *the* maker of phosphorus fertilizer, today! Makes sense to me, if you have a bad economy, people can't afford fertilizer, can they? Wrong! There's an opportunity for you. Wait, a 20 percent decline in the prices of assets in Australia! You know what business they're in down in Australia? Selling raw materials to the Chinese!

Remember the stories about the Chinese? They were going to die on the vine because they were so dependent on selling goods to the United States. That was supposed to happen to the Indians, too. But look what's happened. The Chinese people were hungrier than we are, and were willing to continue to sacrifice immediate comfort to build their society. Moreover, their government, totalitarian though it is, is run by educated people who studied finance and economics in the United States, remember?

Instead of passing out money according to who needs it, (actually, buying the votes of those TV viewers who didn't study economics, just like the politicians they vote for) the Chinese created their own stimulus package. They didn't do it on borrowed money, they used their savings. But they provided rebates for consumers who actually went out and bought something. Instead of bailing out those companies that do a poor job of self-management or try to sell products people don't want to buy, the Chinese government just made it easier for their people to buy the things they want. So *their* stimulus actually stimulated business. Their economy resumed growth and is racing ahead at an 8 percent or 10 percent clip—a growth rate we haven't seen in a hundred years, if ever.

Today we have more opportunity, and the game is more complex. We had to work to sell the American lifestyle piece by piece the first time around. Now everybody in the world is sold on supply-side economics, American ingenuity, and everything about our modern American lifestyle. They want it all. Acceptance of our line of products is so deep royals want to wear Levis. If you are totally awake without preconceptions, this is the world you see.

The world is coming together because of better communication. That means the Internet, high-speed data transfer, and our ability to store gigantic amounts of data on tiny chips and flash memory. It frees our brains, yes, but it also frees the brains of people all over the world. Technology has transformed that one person who used to plow one acre of grain in one field in one day, and gives them control over five machines that do the work of 50 people. All it takes is a little education.

I know. It's tough on the other 49 people, because we don't need them anymore. But they could easily learn to do the same thing, and in the final analysis we produce 10 times more product and make it affordable for everybody. And everybody who educates himself can be involved in moving goods and services all over the world.

That gives them access to TVs, washing machines, computers, and iPods. There's a separate phone number for every member of the family—plus a car for every member of the family and a bathroom for every member of the family. Pretty soon, you're talking about a thousand square feet of house for every member of the family! And no political system, no stock market downturn, nothing is going to stop the educated people all over the world from living like we do. Billions are moving into the middle class, hundreds of millions of those in China alone.

Again we come back to the basic truth we talked about in the previous chapter. We know what those hundreds of millions of people are going to need and that the things they need most will be in short supply. We know that we can make fortunes using our savings and our capital to provide those raw materials and the expertise to use them efficiently. Remember earlier in this chapter when we talked about that MatchBook U grad trying to sell you his life insurance policy? Well, understanding what we're discussing right now, this knowledge, is your real insurance policy.

Let me give you just one good example of what an alternative to that insurance policy might be. In fact, let me tell you what I'm doing in the bond market right now.

Structured Notes, Bonds, and CDs

I'm not always necessarily thrilled with what the markets offer us. There are times when I see a macroeconomic opportunity. Let's say I see an opportunity where I think the market or the rest of the herd has priced the value of a class of assets wrong. At different times, I might see inflation coming, but it isn't yet priced in. I might see other currencies likely to rise in value against the dollar at some point in the future, but the dollar is strong at the moment. I think the prices of some commodities are likely to rise in the future, but they're cheap right now.

At these times, I may be reluctant to make a risky trade based on my beliefs. For one thing, I'm not too clear on the timing. I don't know when the expected change will happen; I just think it will at some point in the coming few years.

Not being too sure about the timing also adds up to risk. For one thing, even though I think metals will eventually rise, they could easily fall in price first. I can be pretty certain that something will be worth more in the future, but that doesn't mean I know when this change will happen, or whether the price will move in the opposite direction first. Also, being fairly certain that some class of assets will eventually appreciate is one thing. Knowing how to pick the bottom tick is quite another. The fact that there are so many ways to lose stops a lot of us from taking advantage of some pretty obvious opportunities for profit.

Here's a great solution, a terrific tool for this type of situation. I get to give up a little of the upside to fashion a much less risky trade. You may have to concentrate a little on this explanation, but I'm confident you'll find this next section to be time (and energy) well spent.

A structured note is essentially a bond. And as I've described them before, a bond in its simplest terms is just a promise. We lend our principle to a financial institution, protected by the full faith and credit of that financial institution, and we get a promise to be repaid. If it's a CD, of course, then there's a little bit more expense associated with that; you don't get quite as good a deal. On the other hand, you have that additional layer of safety up to a certain point, up to $250,000. As with any other CD, you're actually guaranteed return of principle by the FDIC.

So we make this loan to the financial institution. We provide our capital, and they give us a specific date as to when we can redeem that bond or note or CD, and we're looking for somewhere in the two- to four-year range. The bond or note provides for a guaranteed return of my principle at the preset date of maturity, as with any other note or CD. But here's where it's a little different: The interest on my money is calculated based on the performance of some index or the change in price of a certain class of assets.

Of course, we can always take profits on these notes in the open market, so we aren't stuck. And if our strategy is correct, we were not compelled to have guessed the right timing in advance. Now, at that point we have return of principle, and the interest is calculated based on an index.

In June 2009 we saw an opportunity and were able to use this tool to take advantage of it. At the time, the dollar was looking pretty strong, but we expected it to fall in value against some of the other fast-growth currencies around the world. Because the dollar was high at the time, and the markets weren't anticipating the change, it was relatively inexpensive for financial institutions to make the following deal.

We created a three-year note with return of principle guaranteed in three years by the full faith and credit of that financial institution (in this case, Barclays), with the interest to be calculated based upon the change in the value of the dollar versus three currencies: the Chinese yuan, the Russian ruble, and the Canadian dollar. Another note we created was based on the changes in value of the BRIC currencies (Brazil, Russia, India, and China).

Because the prices of options on those assets were favorable at that moment, the formula for calculating the interest worked out to be about double the change in those currencies versus the dollar. That means that if the change in the value of those currencies versus the dollar over that period of time was 10 percent, then we would have a total return of 20 percent. If we had a sudden huge round of inflation in America and the dollar declined by 30 or 40 percent, which I saw as totally possible, then we would have a very large gain as the interest is calculated on that note.

The financial institution bears the responsibility of going out and hedging their position as they see the need. It isn't my problem; I simply have a contract to receive principle and interest based on an agreed-upon formula at some point in the future. And frankly I don't really care how the financial institution goes about protecting itself, that's its job. I'm sure they buy options or futures contracts to hedge our agreement, and they calculate the cost of those instruments into the deal.

They are using derivatives, and I'm using derivatives. I'm not overleveraged. They're not overleveraged. I get to use these instruments to make the exact bet I want to make with the exact level of risk and protection I feel is appropriate. They simply guarantee to pay me an interest rate based upon the performance of a certain index. And then we create the formulas according to what's possible in the market at that time, based upon that financial institution's ability to hedge various situations.

If I happen to be wrong, I still get my principle back, and so I consider this a terrific tool to help me preserve the value of my money, when my country's currency is in danger of falling off the proverbial cliff over the next several years.

Does the word derivative bother you at all? I know it bothers some people. Understand that *derivative* is a word that sends chills up the spines of most people. I want you to get used to that word. Don't react to it as a robot or as a member of the herd. The word derivative just refers to something that's actually made up of something else.

For example, orange juice is a derivative. So are the structured notes I just described. So are convertible bonds, so are warrants that are simply "equity kickers" that we use in the best private deals. So there are mortgage bonds that have made me richer than I ever thought I might be. How? They helped to keep me out of the stock market when almost everybody else on Wall Street was on an eight-year campaign to basically put themselves in the poor house.

The plain truth is I have tools available to me that allow me to make decent—not exciting—but decent money, so I'm able to be very choosy about the stocks I invest in, and I can afford to wait until the moment is just right.

I can patiently wait to deploy my money and take risks when I really, really like the deal—when conditions are ideal and when the time is as right as I can make it. Contrast this with most people, who are in a rush and feel they have to hurry up and buy stocks or mutual funds because they're running out of time. If they're in a rush, they'll rush to judgment, and that's the ultimate case of what I call very poor timing. A regular equity investment or a futures market trade requires a level of precision that makes the odds of winning much lower than the odds of eventually being right.

So now a fair question might be, "How do you find these macro-economic strategic notes and CDs?" I can sometimes negotiate a deal with investment banks like Barclays Bank and Goldman Sachs. Sometimes I can find these notes and CDs out there in the secondary market, a place where *you* can actually go out and buy them, because they're left over from a deal done by some institutional investor (like me). I see them on the Web all the time. One website available to everybody, where they list hundreds of these structured notes, is BondsOnLine.

Here's where you get paid big money as though you took a lot of risk, but all you've really done was your required homework, just as my grandfather promised me 50 years ago. You have to be very careful. You have to know what you're doing, and you have to read THE FINE PRINT, because sometimes the *way* these notes are structured can be very deceptive.

Whenever we can't find exactly what we're looking for, we'll actually create such a deal in collaboration with somebody like Barclays Bank. If you don't have a few million to invest at a time, you can't do it this way, but I want you to know that it's going on out there, and I assure you, you *can* find the right people to help you. But be on your toes, and don't check your brain at the door.

So now you have a choice. You can (a) give your money to the representatives and salesmen from struggling financial institutions, buying guarantees from them to provide you money when you need it, investing in the wrong things just because you're used to them. Or you can (b) invest your money in the things you're used to, promoted by the leaders you're used to following, and using the same old habits you've been comfortable with. If you choose (a) or (b), I'd say you'd better buy a lot of insurance to go with it. What I'd suggest is that you (c) take responsibility, use your capital to help people get what they want, make a lot of money, and provide for your own old age. Here again, responsibility means power.

Back a couple of years ago, the problem was that the strategy of buying these materials companies was obvious—everybody was doing it so the risk was very high, because their prices were bid up very high. Now we get the low-risk entry point to take these positions again, and you don't have to be dependent on what happens in your neighborhood, your town, or even what happens in the United States. You don't have to allow your fortune to depend on our economic growth or our stock market. You can join me. We can make our own way, create our own boom, and bring as many people along with us as we can reach. It's unbelievably easy, once you know that the negative, myopic, short-term news being transmitted to the herd via TV, radio, newspapers, and the Internet is totally missing the point.

All of us will be swayed, influenced, and scared, but we can fight to stay awake. We can write down our strategy now, while we can see it, and understand it, and read it every day. The symphony of short-term negative myopia will fill our environment. It will not make us feel like making the right investments. It will frighten us right at the point of taking that risk, like a quarterback about to throw that long ball. Sure he's afraid, but it's a fear filled with energy. And he's learned to turn that energy into power. He knows happiness isn't won by succumbing to fear. Happiness comes from leaving everything on the field.

3

The Media Act

You Can't Believe Everything You Read or Hear or See

In this chapter...

- Analyst: "There's a slowdown. No, there's not! Yes there is..."
- The media act like priests
- You're not stupid; the Emperor *was* naked
- No money, no jobs, no sales, no profits—whew!
- And what happened? Why, it's like there are 6 billion Americans!

It's All Psycho-Babble

There are few winners and hundreds of millions of losers. List the winners, and you'll find that many of them started with nothing and made themselves ultra-rich and ultra-famous on pure brain power and determination. If you're not a winner, it's only because you have certain tendencies. We all have them. Stop succumbing to them and you'll be rich. How do I know? Because the world is literally brimming with opportunity and resources. Look around you.

But why believe your eyes? Why believe me? The media tells you just the opposite, and they're so compelling! How can you tell who's right? How can you be confident? Here's a quote from a highly paid professional stock analyst and commentator from one of the major brokerage houses—a respected company (now defunct, by the way).

I was on the set with him one day and I had trouble believing what I was hearing. As he was speaking, I was reminded of that story about the naked Emperor.

Here's what he said:

> *"Until I see the catalyst, I say we're still in a bear-market rally—one to be enjoyed right up until the last moment, but a bear-market rally nevertheless. And I continue to worry that we have already seen "the last moment"—at least for a while. The bulls have become too emboldened. It seems too easy again. The markets need to correct the gains of the past month and see if there's really anyone there to buy when all of these supposed bargains get even better. We're not going overboard, not jumping into second-tier tech and not loading up" on equities, he said. "But you don't want to fight with this market because the worst thing would be to get far behind the benchmark index and get handcuffed, because if you're wrong, you're going to lose your job."*

If these comments sound like doubletalk to you, I quite agree. I'm withholding the name of the analyst who said this junk, because I'm not out to attack or destroy any particular person; I'm sure the guy's just trying to make a living. He's still out there, and people who admire him are still losing money, but I'm here to help you acquire the wisdom to take you to a much higher level.

Let me tell you how it happened that anyone was able to write such junk, pass it off on thousands or millions of unsuspecting followers, and probably cause enough financial losses to equal an amount that could bail a small country out of recession.

These people are in a business. Their job is to sell one specific service. They know millions of Americans are stuck in the '90s, and they want to jump in front of the herd and look like the leaders. They want to do this because leaders (or experts—whatever you want to call them) get paid for playing with *your* money, instead of risking their own.

Now, let's really evaluate and understand those experts. You're smart enough to evaluate ideas on their own merits, instead of taking the lazy man's shortcut and looking for a leader you can trust. You're certainly aware that finding leaders and accepting their ideas takes much less energy, but you've learned where that gets you; I can almost see you evolving as you're reading this.

The analyst I referred to earlier is in the public trust because he is one of many who are famous, and who are famous simply because they get the *ink*. I get a little ink myself, and I see these guys on various panels and TV shows, hanging out in the green rooms sharing a lot of this double-talk over coffee. These are the guys who in late 2007 were saying, "Slowdown? What slowdown? Show it to me. Look at the government numbers. The economy is fine."

Personally, I was engaged in several debates about this very subject on CNBC and Fox Business, as well as on my radio program. I can still hear them: "Where's the slowdown? Look at the GDP figures! Look at the gains in employment!" Then in 2008, I was hearing a very different story: "This will be a mild and quick recession that won't affect consumers." As of this writing, Ben Bernanke is the current Fed chairman. You can count him in this group, by the way. I don't know how much further off a forecast can be, yet just today, as I write this chapter, I see Chairman Bernanke's latest forecasts moving the market again.

I could continue with a litany of foolish analysis, but the previous quote in this chapter says it all for me, and I know for a fact I'm not the first to notice this phenomenon. This is exactly what the ancient story of the naked emperor is about—his subjects pretending to believe he was wearing clothes to avoid being looked upon as incompetent, rather than saying what they knew to be true, what they could see with their own eyes, that the man was *naked* for crying out loud! Whoever wrote that story would have easily understood exactly how this analyst has been able to maintain a following with that kind of analysis. The audience is hard-wired to believe whatever they see treated with respect on TV.

This is one of your experts, stuck in a habit of thinking a certain way, totally incapacitated because he is operating strictly on memory and habitual beliefs—a virtual robot. The real opportunities to make big money in the market come at major turning points. Yet, these people must eventually help you lose your money as soon as you reach one of those turning points, because their method is to make decisions based on past memories. Then, just to be safe, they leave a small margin for a little uncertainty.

Extrapolation only works when things continue in their current direction. With major changes afoot, being stuck in the past can only confuse you. You must free your mind to look forward, not backward.

What these guys *don't* know is so much more than what they *do* know about the future, that their preconceptions and biases cause them to completely miss the point when the future is different from the past. How much money was lost in 2008 because of this errant tendency, and how much potential profit was never made by investors in 2009?

When the banking system froze up and business virtually stopped, looking at previous history and adjusting your expectations downward by 20 percent or 30 percent, well, that's crazy. In an economy that isn't functioning and people can't get financing to do business, profits don't decline incrementally, they *stop*, they go to zero!

This is just common sense, yet this cadre of influential analysts dropped their estimates a little bit every month based on their previous estimates and were totally wrong 15 times in a row. A company making zero profit or losing money has a much different value than a company that makes 20 percent less profit than it did last year. If anyone kept track of their batting averages, they'd be gone from our lives. They wouldn't be on TV. They wouldn't be advising thousands, or even hundreds. They wouldn't be advising anybody.

OK, so you can understand how people could be confused enough to listen to these guys in the '80s and '90s. Prices of all investments were rising anyway, and following the experts' advice was profitable. How could anyone know that the advice was irrelevant? That's all understandable, but what about today? As we close in on the end of this first decade of the millennium, it's clear that anyone who has been following this advice has lost half of his/her net worth. Both the givers and the receivers of this advice are totally confused. Actually the givers of the advice get paid to do it, so I guess they aren't that confused. But you have to ask yourself, "What are the people thinking who continue to act on this advice after it has proven less valuable than a coin flip so consistently."

We're back to the question I've been asking myself for over 40 years: "What is that lemming saying to itself, as it follows its leader over that cliff?" At age 64, my theory is this: Neither of them is thinking at all.

We're about to get into a very important area. And I know you've already read the analyst's comment, but bear with me because I want you to read it again. Don't skip over it. This is an important exercise, and understanding it is the key to the following observation.

"Until I see the catalyst, I say we're still in a bear-market rally—one to be enjoyed right up until the last moment, but a bear-market rally nevertheless. And I continue to worry that we have already seen "the last moment"—at least for a while. The bulls have become too emboldened. It seems too easy again. The markets need to correct the gains of the past month and see if there's really anyone there to buy when all of these supposed bargains get even better. We're not going overboard, not jumping into second-tier tech and not loading up" on equities, he said. "But you don't want to fight with this market because the worst thing would be to get far behind the benchmark index and get handcuffed, because if you're wrong, you're going to lose your job."

Why are these guys still in place? How could this guy still be influential and well paid? I think it's because we are hardwired to follow the priests, the arbiters of truth. These media analysts are our new priesthood. I see you looking at me funny for using the term "priesthood." I'm going to explain it, and in so doing, you're about to see why I wanted to drill that previous quote into your brain. Now before I say anything else, please, *please* take heed of my disclaimer:

I am hereby taking no position whatsoever on my beliefs or yours about creation, the creator, how we got to this universe or where we go next. Like you, I have no proof or answers to those questions. I know no more about it than you do, and the issue is totally beside my point. Any conclusion you reach about anything after taking the responsibility to think it through is just fine by me.

The Priesthood

You're probably aware that when society was first organizing thousands of years ago, the first class of people that arose to live off of everyone else's labors was the priesthood. It was their job to define the habits of the gods to the people—to communicate the wishes of the gods to the frightened, helpless herd. Bear in mind, the flock was not looking for religion. They were looking for real answers: "Say, how do you make it rain, so we can survive; if it's all up to the gods, how do we get 'em to cooperate?"

If you stop to think about it, when we make references to religion, we're talking about things that we don't really believe—or more accurately, the things we have to work hard to believe. Science is what we call our state-of-the-art beliefs, things that we consider proven. Of course, when we're thinking clearly, we know that science isn't quite that pat either. It seems that every few years we find out that some things we were once positive about are either wrong or incomplete. In other words, what we call science isn't necessarily exact or perfectly correct either, but it's what we believe to be true.

When we refer to our religion, we're talking about things that take a bit of faith to believe in. Simply stated, religion is about things we doubt, science is about things we firmly believe. Once you see this, you can understand the role of the priests. They're pretty much a go-between, standing between us and our own personal God, explaining to us how the world works. The group we actually call "priests" (the ones over at the actual church) has very little real power in our society. They preside over those things we doubt. This is very important, so I want you to really get it. You are in the process of freeing yourself to be rich.

Let's face it, no priest in America could ever actually get somebody to sacrifice their first born. You have to really get it that 10,000 years ago people were physically and psychologically very much like you and me. And those people routinely sacrificed their first born to the gods in order to get good weather for agriculture. Obviously, to them, this was science. They had to believe in it pretty firmly to make such a huge sacrifice. It represented their state-of-the-art understanding of nature and the universe.

That, too, is the role of the media's so-called financial experts. It's the same thinking that's helped to set up and maintain the role of the experts on child rearing, guys like Dr. Phil. These arbiters of truth, these people who lead our thinking occupy the same place in our society as the priesthood did 10,000 years ago.

Now here's the ironic ending to this part of the tale, and in my book (which, coincidentally, this is) it's a happy ending: Finally, after all the years I've been around Wall Street, the broker community finally started to *believe* their own hype and to take their own advice. Look what happened to them! And it's what's been happening to their followers and customers as long as I've been alive.

So now that you understand, what do you do about it? Avoid all commentary? Stay away from financial media? If I felt that way, I wouldn't be as actively involved in financial broadcasting as I am. What I'm suggesting is that you listen *critically* to the commentary. I mean actually *listen* to it. If you think you're going to act on it, record it. Listen to it a few times. Transcribe it and then read it—make sure it makes sense to you.

Most importantly, understand that we humans are hard-wired to evaluate leaders, not ideas. If you can find a person you trust, you only have to make the judgment once, and then you can get thousands of ideas from that source. But you don't really progress or evolve into what we've come to call Investor 2.0 until the day you decide to evaluate each of that guy's *ideas*. The dumbest person can be right sometimes, and the smartest person can be wrong. Your only shot is to evaluate the ideas, one at a time. Hey, sometimes the emperor's dressed, and maybe sometimes he really is naked. You'll never know unless your eyes *and* your mind are open. And I don't want to pressure you, but people you love are depending on you. Evolve. And start now!

So What Do the Winners Do?

Well, now, welcome back to the land of the living. For a little while, at least, you're not a robot. You're not thinking like a lemming. As the movie trailer guy says, "In a world of robots and lemmings, you don't have to follow *anyone* over a cliff." And hey, he's right; you're free to create the life you want. If I were you, I'd mark this chapter and come back to it often—maybe every time you start to think about your investments.

Instead of aimlessly searching for some priest, or guru, or expert to do your thinking for you, here's a simple step-by-step process. It's basically the process great investors like Steven Schwarzman of The Blackstone Group use. Schwarzman, by the way, was the highest paid executive in the United States last year at around $700 million.

Just start from scratch and build your own strategy, undistorted by the pull of the herd. You're about to become your own leader. You're about to start thinking like a billionaire. I can tell you from experience, the big money will follow. Here then, are a couple of simple steps to devising your own strategy instead of following the lead lemmings. At the same time, I'll also give you some in-depth directions on how to get them right. Ready? Here we go.

First, forecast future events using vision instead of extrapolation. Consider tactical moves and adjust your forecast based on your estimate of their success. How confident are you in your forecast? Make a realistic assessment of the chances that you're wrong. WARNING:

Those chances are definitely not zero. This is the step the big boys never miss, and the amateurs almost never take. If you think your stock or your company could double in value over the next three years, but you see a 30 percent chance of being wrong, that's not a better investment than a company with a very high chance of success that makes 20 percent a year. This kind of thinking won't make every deal you do come out right, but it'll mean the difference between rich and poor.

The reason most of us miss this obvious common-sense step is that common sense has been completely removed from the process of judging risk. The whole middle-class retail investors' world, the financial planners' world, and the world of finance as studied at a university is based on an idea that is totally wrong: Financial planning, as it is practiced today, starts with this idea: Let risk equal volatility.

This is the concept that lost you all your money, and you didn't even know it. That whole religion we talked about earlier—the Modern Portfolio Theory—was based on this errant idea. Economists won Nobel prizes for the idea that they could measure risk accurately by measuring volatility. Once you get past the very shortest time frame, trading in minutes and hours, this idea is totally wrong. Risk is not synonymous with volatility. Risk is the chance of you being wrong and losing money. Volatility only serves to describe vibrations. It's meaningless, except when it comes to time frames so short that price movements are unrelated to any changes in the value of assets. Then, volatility or vibrations are all that matter.

Take a company like Cisco Systems. I don't care if Cisco Systems stock tends to fluctuate in the short term. This only tells me that the stock is traded a lot by people with a very short-term view, who really don't care about using their capital to make a meaningful contribution to humanity.

Cisco Systems is miles ahead of every possible competitor, controlling the entire world industry of allowing computers and other high-tech devices to communicate with each other. If any company becomes a meaningful competitor in any part of this industry, Cisco simply buys them. As the world becomes one through electronic communication, Cisco stands alone as the dominant facilitator. There's high volatility, but almost zero chance of failure! Volatility does not equal risk.

Now consider the fact that our government is adding something like 12 trillion paper dollars to the world economy, while producing no product of value. This tells me the dollar has a good chance of falling in value (being able to buy you less stuff) over the next several years. Your Treasury Bonds and savings accounts are denominated in dollars, right? So if the dollar falls in value, you get poorer. There's low volatility, but a high likelihood of loss. Risk does not equal volatility.

Which one seems riskier in the long run: that volatile Cisco stock or those nice, tame U.S. Treasuries? How much money have you already missed out on by blindly following those Nobel Prize-winning money-losers who foolishly believe in making investment choices based on the size of the vibrations, rather than basing choices on the substance of the investments and insights about future profits, and estimating the odds of success or failure? Consider carefully the following idea: *The value of an investment to you as an investor is the future cash flow, adjusted for the probability of being wrong, less the tax.*

It's easy to find it in the writings of such geniuses as Arthur Laffer and John Rutledge, but it doesn't help sell insurance, so it never gets to most people. If you get *this* idea, you'll be halfway to a life of wealth and comfort. It's simple, but crucial, so here it is again: *The value of an investment to you as an investor is the future cash flow, adjusted for the probability of being wrong, less the tax.*

This is where the deal becomes interesting to the winning investor. When there is a big enough difference between the current market price and the value to you, you've found a good deal. Now, all you have to do is compare this opportunity to your other opportunities, and you have a great chance to come out a winner.

So why is it so difficult for us to think independently? How have we been blindsided by events that seem so obvious now? It's really not that difficult to get an edge over a mindless herd of lemmings. Most of us don't see a tsunami coming because this type of independent thinking just doesn't come naturally to humans. And, by the way, that's just peachy for those of us who can free ourselves from the hypnosis of the herd. When we do, we bump into lots of opportunity and weak competition—what in the Marine Corps we used to call a target-rich environment.

We're not automatically equipped for today's quick changes because in terms of our natural instincts and our physical abilities we're very much like our ancestors of half a million years ago. Back then, things changed very slowly. The world stayed very much the same for thousands of years at a time, so the fittest among our ancestors were the people who inherited the ability and the tendency to learn from the past. They saved time and beat out the competition by assuming their past experience would be applicable to the next hunt or the next migration.

How then does this tendency translate into the strategic errors that cost you and your neighbors trillions of dollars? For one thing, millions of investors around the world rely on earnings forecasts by the experts to formulate their investment strategy. I'm sure you know that, but here's something you don't know: Not one person who relies on analysts' earnings forecasts has made any real money in many, many years—not one. For every win, they suffer several defeats, because at the critical turning points, the past does not help foretell the future.

Table 3.1 is provided by my friend, John Mauldin. Take a look at the monthly adjustments made by the corps of sell-side analysts each month, as they incorrectly forecasted the earnings for the S & P 500 all through 2008.

Ask yourself what methodology could lead the top professional earnings analysts to be so wrong so many times in a row? Flipping a coin would make you right half the time; what kind of methodology could make you wrong 12 times in a row?

Then ask yourself, how could so many of these errant analysts still be working, still be paid a lot of money, and how could you and millions of others still be relying on them to help you devise

Table 3.1   **Falling Earnings Estimates for the S&P 500 for 2008**

Date	Earnings
March 2007	$92
December 2007	$84
February 2008	$71.20
June 1, 2008	$68.93
July 25, 2008	$72.01
September 30, 2008	$60
October 15, 2008	$54.82

Source: John Mauldin.

your strategies for the future? The earnings analysts' methodology is simple. They start with what they know, which is the past. Since they know their knowledge isn't complete, they make an adjustment to the past numbers based on how good or bad they feel at the moment. And then, because they want to allow for uncertainty, they add a 10 percent or 20 percent adjustment for what they don't know.

I'll repeat what I said before, and now you'll understand why it's so important. *What they know is dwarfed by what they don't know; therefore it's totally crazy to base their expectations on what they know.* At major turning points, which happen more and more frequently in modern times, a 10 percent or 20 percent adjustment to the past is a joke.

By 2008, everything about the United States *and* global economy had changed. Sales and profits were going from good to zero—no money, no jobs, no capital, no refinancing, no sales, no profit. It's as simple as that. Past success was totally irrelevant. In the past, consumers were buying, companies had financing, and the economy was functioning normally. In 2008, everything was grinding to a not-so-gradual halt.

Yet analysts looked at the previous year's earnings, and asked themselves out loud on TV: "Do you think profits could actually be down 50 percent? I've never seen that in my life, so let's say they decline by 30 percent. That would be huge!" Does that sound like science to you? Of course, they were totally wrong. When people stop buying, you don't get a 20 percent decline. You go from up to down! Just evaluating the situation from the top down—just thinking instead of remembering—was a much better technique. Looking forward would have taken brain cells; making those incorrect estimates used memory cells. Think about it.

So what does freedom to think for yourself do for you? Well, if you don't mind, I'll share *my* current thinking. Everyone is waiting for the U.S. economy to recover, and waiting for the growth of the past 30 years to resume. They base this expectation on the fact that, in their memory, it has always worked this way—a year or two of recession, leading to three or four years of recovery.

Americans are eager for the all-clear to sound. They want to invest in the retail recovery, the manufacturing recovery, the technology recovery, and, well, you name it. Millions are just waiting for the go-ahead from the TV gurus to get started. Others are just tired of being disappointed; they trust no one and do nothing, and are out of the market, period. Still others are following advice they absorbed from hearing so many times over the past 30 years: "Keep at least 10 percent of your money overseas for diversification."

I see more opportunity to make money today than at any time in my life, because I do everything I can to keep myself awake and to free myself. I keep reminding myself that I have no beliefs. My success will be based on using my brains instead of my memory, because I insist on looking forward instead of backward.

Six Billion (gulp) Americans? What's Changed?

What's changed? Oh, that's easy.

- The United States used to be the largest lender on the planet.
- Every country in the world owed the United States money.
- Virtually every major invention and technology originated and was centered in the United States.
- Other countries relied on central planning, giving us a huge competitive advantage.
- "Made in the U.S.A." meant quality; made overseas meant junk, especially in Asia.
- The oceans surrounded us, protected our society, and insulated us from other cultures.
- Communication between us and other cultures was expensive and tedious.

The best and the brightest from everywhere in the world migrated to the United States in search of opportunity, and they almost invariably stayed and settled here. U.S. business constantly renewed itself and evolved through survival of the fittest. We laughed at other countries, which were too mired in the past to allow their industries to renew themselves. The United States was home to the baby boomers, a gigantic contingent of people in the prime of their lives. Baby boomers were totally focused on productivity, entrepreneurship, consumption, new business investment, new infrastructure spending, and risk-taking.

Do you think anything has changed? Do you think your strategies of the past, with a 10 or 20 percent adjustment, will take you where you want to go? Today's world is evolving so fast that any list of anything that's devised today will probably be obsolete before this book can be printed, but let me give it a try.

- American kids at our best universities are totally intimidated. They say they can't get into medical schools because the seats are all being taken up by international students.
- The United States is the largest *borrower* of money on the planet.
- I see an aging baby-boom population in the United States, a poorly conceived economic and fiscal policy in the United States, and that's likely to move capital investment out of our country for a long, long time.
- At the same time, I see demographics, fiscal policy, and economic growth persisting in China and in the rest of Asia, as countries in that hemisphere feed materials and labor to a growing, increasingly transparent, and well-managed China.
- I see a China that is continuing to support the U.S. economy by lending us money, but working as hard as they can to free themselves from dependence on exports, and to develop industries based on Chinese selling to Chinese.

For me, those anachronistic 10 percent rules should be thrown right into your round file, right now. I'd even stop considering which country a company considers its home. The question to consider is how plugged in is it to the growth story for the next 10 years? It's actually not difficult; it just doesn't come naturally to humans to think this way. Again, if you think about it, that's just peachy for those of us who master this skill. There's lots of opportunity and lots of weak competition. Sound familiar?

Simplicity = Apple + Π

So, what country is home to Apple Computers? Frankly, who cares? What difference would it make? Of course, you know Apple is the quintessential American company. It encompasses much of what the world loves about the United States, and the truth is, I don't think anybody else could have created anything so cool and, well, American as Apple. I mean, think of it: the Big Apple, apple pie, baseball, Chevrolet—c'mon, you know the drill. And there's no U.S.-based company that is truly benefiting from a world without economic borders more than the folks behind the door that boasts the famous green apple: Apple Inc. (AAPL).

Well, that goes to show how impressionable we all are. See? I automatically knew it was a green apple. But just to be sure, I just Googled "Apple" and clicked on the very first link, right there at the top. Yes, it did indeed take me to an Apple site, actually the official Apple store, but no matter how hard I looked, I couldn't find that darned green apple logo. In fact, I clicked through six pages before I found any apple at all, and it was red! *And* it had a bite taken out of it!

Frustrated, and knowing I wasn't completely crazy, I Googled "Apple *Logo*." Ah-ha! So there's the green apple! It's right there, along with the red one, the glitzy chrome-looking one, and the horizontally striped rainbow version. Yes, yes, I know. When you see an apple, any apple, you better believe it's nobody *but* Apple. Next to Coca-Cola, it's probably the most recognized logo in the world. And they're so big and so well-known, they no longer even feel like they need to tout the logo, at least not for the first five or six pages. Talk about brand recognition—Apple's a monster.

This $153 billion company designs, manufactures, and markets personal computers, portable digital music players, and mobile communication devices—and sells a variety of related software, services, peripherals, and networking solutions. Apple sells its products worldwide through its online stores, retail stores, direct sales force, and third-party wholesalers, resellers, and value-added resellers. In addition, the company sells a variety of third-party Macintosh (Mac), iPod, and iPhone compatible products, including application software, printers, storage devices, speakers, headphones, and various other accessories and peripherals. All of this is through its online and retail stores, plus digital content through the iTunes Store.

Apple sells to the consumer, small- and mid-sized business (SMB), education, enterprise, government, and creative customers. But you know what makes Apple different than most companies trying to squeeze into this space? It's the fact that they actually make products people around the world want and need. The iPod changed the way the world listened to music. This enabled Apple to grab a whole new set of customers for their computers. The invention of the iPhone did the same thing for the smart phone market. And they're not resting; In 2010, it is rumored that Apple is planning to unveil a tablet that could change the personal computing market forever! These people innovate!

In a U.S. economy that will struggle to grow over the next several years, Apple is not relying on debt or the U.S. government for its growth. Its unique innovations and products make it truly a dominant company in the technology space, and despite the company's legendary success, they are almost unknown in China right now. In China, the next big thing is the iPhone, and the Chinese telephone companies are having to subsidize its distribution. Most Chinese people aren't used to spending that kind of money for a phone. But they will, won't they? You bet.

Like the entire technology sector, more than half of Apple's sales come from outside the United States of America. That's key for an American company, due to the long-term pressure on the U.S. dollar.

And look, I could run you pages and pages of numbers and statistics to show you just how solid a company Apple has become. On the other hand you can find those numbers and statistics anywhere. Let me just state very simply that Apple, Inc. (AAPL) has sales growth over 35 percent and a return on equity over 25 percent. Their margins are remarkably strong, and with new customers being added everyday—all around the world—they provide us a terrific way to help people get what they want. Like you and me, the brand new middle-class Asians, Africans, and Latin Americans are going to go after what they want, long before they get what they need.

4

Cashing in on Six Billion Opportunities

Decision-Making 2.0

I n this chapter...

- Play for the love of the game and win. Play for the love of others, get snookered by Chi Chi.
- Think rich and get rich? No, think smart and get rich.
- High emotions don't last—not even on the Crisis Hotline.
- Decide by making decisions; Read and learn, even if the rest of the library's empty.
- Make decisions like a Marine, or a chess player: Go on your gut, use your instinct.

Transactional Analysis—Wires in Your Brain

Years ago I read a book about transactional analysis. It's really a very simple idea. Part of it has to do with well-known research. Psychologists have found that they can stimulate certain parts of your brain with electrodes and you see things from your past so clearly that you actually believe they're happening right now. You can smell things, taste things, even if they're not really there. By stimulating the right part of your brain you can hear music as though it was there. For me, understanding the concept helped me to become mentally free, allowing me to make money on Wall Street.

Here's how it works: It seems that every impression and every experience you've ever had is stored in your brain, much of it below the level of consciousness. There are different parts of you there because of impressions you have of yourself as a child. On the one hand there's an angry, frustrated child. On the other hand, there's a happy, carefree child who's being treated lovingly and made secure by his parents. There are also impressions of what you believed your parents thought of this child. And even if you were wrong in what you *thought* they thought, you still carry it around with you.

If you want to understand some of the distortions in our subconscious and the parents we carry around with us in our brains, picture this: A three-year-old child is with his mother walking down the street. The child turns and starts to run into the street. There's heavy traffic, and in a panic, the mother chases the child, grabs his arm as tight as she can, jerks him back onto the sidewalk, smacks him, and gives him a good scolding about what-for. As adults, you and I understand this experience perfectly. We know that the mother isn't really angry at the child. She was simply afraid—worried, trying to protect the child, afraid that she hasn't taught him well enough. The mother is only really expressing love for the child, but the child sees an angry, judgmental parent.

When you were that age, everything you did was cute and everything you did was wonderful and your parents doted on you and gave you nothing but approval and unconditional love. And then somewhere along the line, they suddenly started to think it's high time for you to control your bathroom functions. For the first time it turns out that there are some things you do that your parents *don't* approve of.

Of course they think it's their job to acculturate you, to teach you, to socialize you. But from your viewpoint as a child, well, just imagine the first time that you would have seen disapproval from those parents. Imagine that first moment when the child comes to the stark realization, "Hey wait a minute. These people seem to love some of the stuff I do and they're not too crazy about other stuff... hmmm." Now, depending on how that moment went, that could have been a moment of enormous pain and trauma.

Many of us walk around with that internal parent inside us all the time. Even if our parents are no longer anywhere near us, even if they're no longer living, here we are still walking around rehearsing conversations with them and feeling their approval or disapproval.

Of course, as a child, the parent that we mentally carry around may be absolutely nothing like the actual parent that we have—it's just the impression of a child, the image that you had of your parents as a two-, three-, or four-year-old. But if you have this overactive parent inside you, then it's affecting your decision-making.

Getting Snookered by Chi Chi

As part of an interview a few years ago, I played a round of golf with Chi Chi Rodriguez. I'd asked him that day, "How early did you become a professional?" He said, "Well, growing up in Puerto Rico, my family was broke. I never had the luxury of being an amateur; I always had to play for money." Turns out that Chi Chi was a caddy at a golf course for tourists in Puerto Rico. And, of course, the caddies get to play the course all the time. And they get pretty good. And some of them get really, really, *really* good. Chi Chi was, of course, one of the best—a very talented and gifted golfer.

But he was always looking for a mark, someone to hustle—even at seven, eight, nine years old. I understand that experience perfectly because I was a sort of caddy at the NYSE at that age. Chi Chi knew what he was looking for; he was looking for a loser, a sucker. He'd be out there carrying the guys' clubs and advising the guys on the course; he'd be giving guys ideas about what club to use and what to watch out for. But he was watching, too. Because when they got onto the greens, just like most golfers (even the good ones), they would inevitably make a lousy putt. They'd miss putts that they really should have made.

What Chi Chi was looking for was the guy who, when he missed the putt, would look around at the other guys to see who might have noticed. Chi Chi's looking for the guy who was more interested in the approval of his fellow golfers than he was in making a good score. *That* was the guy who would end up as the mark for Chi Chi Rodriguez.

The whole point is that looking for approval distorts your response; it takes away your ability to be unconsciously competent; it has you imposing other irrelevant factors; and it makes you a bad player, especially when you're playing against the greats. This, my friend, goes right to the whole idea of making the right decisions—because if you're trying to win love rather than trying to win because you're playing for money, it's going to make you weak every time. You can't win if you have that kind of weakness. And every strong player is looking for that weakness in his opponent.

How Do You "Think Rich"? Simple, You Just Think!

Every success-motivation book, seminar, and late-night infomercial tells you that the secret to success is to create and take responsibility. In short, THINK RICH! The problem with that whole industry and that line of thinking, while it's totally true, is that it's only helpful to, and in fact it only works for, the people who already have the gift and know how to use it. For everyone else, it sounds good, but they can't move because they don't know where to start. What it means to me is "take a crack at every great opportunity." Right in the middle of the worst stock market crash since the great depression, I saw a way to make a great profit with very little risk by substituting brains and homework for high risk. I saw my chance to help people get what they want, and get paid very well for doing it. So I went for it.

You could almost hear the spooky music track in the background; everybody was cowering in fear. The financial engineers that everyone had always looked up to (specifically the U.S. Treasury secretary and the Fed chairman) had made some terrible decisions. They saw bad things happening—problems caused directly by their decisions. They had a natural tendency to cover them up, or compensate, or at least try to figure out how to make the whole mess come out better. Their motivations were honorable, I'm sure. They're brilliant guys, right? Just trying to do their best.

Well, at precisely that moment in time—I don't know, maybe Jupiter aligned with Mars or something— I was fortunate enough to be running back and forth doing what we call TV hits (little mini interviews) on the floors of the CME in Chicago, the NYSE in New York, in the FOX Studios, and in the CNBC studios. And by the way I was also running a prime-time financial radio talk show. I basically had a front-row seat right on the 50-yard-line for the whole drama.

Remember now, the rest of the world around me was hiding in the corner with a blanket over their heads. They were afraid, afraid and not willing to risk any money on anything. There was virtually no thinking or strategizing going on anywhere, just highly emotional, knee-jerk reactions. They call this a flight to safety. It's the same kind of flight-to-safety mentality that fish have as the fisherman drives them into a net.

The U.S. government was offering financial support to any institution that asked for it. The market was full of ultra-high-quality corporate bonds that were being sold at large discounts by anyone who had to raise cash, but there were few takers. The spread between U.S. Treasuries and high-grade corporate bonds was huge. Municipal bonds, too, were being sold at historically unprecedented discounts. The low prices meant extra-high current yields, all for just using your head instead of your emotions and taking no particular risk.

But armed with the right information, you would have known that these municipal bonds were protected by the full faith and credit of affluent states such as Texas and Tennessee. States with low tax rates, excellent revenue bases, and with the certainty (at least to me) that the feds stand prepared to back them should the need arise.

Without even having to predict whether interest rates in general would move up or down, it was clear that the unbelievably large spread between Treasuries and these high grade, but less understood bonds would soon narrow. The *fear trade* was simple. Any regular guy can sell Treasuries short via the Exchange Traded Fund. The costs are minimal, and you can even do it with IRA or other retirement plan money.

Also, any regular guy or gal, any average Joe, can buy high-grade corporate bonds and high-grade municipals. The outcome is pretty clear, and we've done exactly what I learned from my grandfather more than half a century ago: We get paid for taking risk, and all we had to do was think clearly and do our homework.

So if it's not clear to you yet, let me say it out loud: If you're looking for an easy and profitable life, and you want to take advantage of the immense opportunities this global economy offers by staying awake and continuing to learn and exercise your brain, this book is perfect for you. If you don't believe we're in a new world that requires new knowledge and skill, and you're hoping to be able to go back to operating on memory, I'd put the book down and go back to reading the free literature your insurance man or financial planner is passing out. This assumes of course that he or she is not out of business and currently driving a cab.

Crisis Hotline—The Back-Story

Anything that makes sense to someone only when they're completely overtaken with emotion cannot last, because as I learned as a kid working the Crisis Hotline in the '80s, people never stay in a state of peak emotion for very long. They will either regain normal consciousness or kill each other. They just aren't capable of maintaining that high level of emotion for months at a time.

There was one time in particular that I remember very well. It was around 1980; I was working nights, and there was a full moon. I was on duty at the Crisis Hotline, taking calls anonymously from troubled citizens. It was late, and a woman called, screaming. It took a minute or two, but I finally figured out that her husband was threatening to commit suicide. I got him to join us on the other extension. Now they start screaming at each other. I don't remember what the fight was about, but she kept yelling, "Stop him!" I muted the phone and looked around, frantically looking for somebody, anybody—to call the police, trace the address, something! My supervisors tried to suppress the situation, reminding me that I'd promised not to get involved in these people's lives and to keep everything anonymous. "What? Are you crazy? Don't you get it, your rules don't matter. This guy's gonna kill himself!"

One of the senior supervisors came over, a fellow in suspenders holding an unlit pipe. He calmly explained to me that by the time we traced the call and got police to them, the crisis would be over. I asked him how he could be so sure. "Humans just can't stay in that heightened state for long. They'll either get tired of it or kill themselves. I know, I know, but either way, a situation that intense can only persist for a few minutes." Well, I have to be honest, I didn't really buy it, but I couldn't do anything about it. And as it turned out, the supervisor was right. I was still on the phone, listening as they finally got tired of the battle; they stopped yelling at each other, and we said goodbye. I hung up. Nothing was settled. The frantic moment just simply ended.

Obviously the first rule is to avoid getting yourself emotionally caught up in the situation. This knowledge has made me a lot of money over the years, and it can work for you as well. Seldom is a frantic reaction to a frantic situation helpful. Just think about your own intense fights with your spouse or your friends. Note how quickly the wild emotion passes. Usually, as crucial as it may feel when you're making fools of yourselves, you simply end the drama without really settling anything.

I knew, as you will soon come to understand, that these high-intensity flights to quality always end with relaxing tension and diminishing volatility. That doesn't mean I know how any episode will end, only that the high anxiety of the moment will dissipate, and more rational relationships will resume between classes of investments. As emotions relax and investors wake up, they realize how dumb they are to limit their investments to Treasuries, when they would trust their state and huge corporations with their money in a hundred ways every day. As they wake up, they'll usually start talking to themselves: "Was I nuts? Settling for 2 percent by lending my money to the government for 10 years? I would have been more than willing to extend commercial credit to the State of Texas or to the Phillip Morris Company anytime they asked! How could I have been so crazy?"

By doing the trade from both sides—long corporates and short Treasuries—I don't have to predict how the intense situation will resolve itself, only that it will resolve. By buying the devalued, beaten-down corporate or munis, and selling the too-high-priced Treasuries, I'm betting only on the narrowing of the spread, not predicting in which direction the resolution will come. You have to do both sides to eliminate the need for fortune telling. The bet is on human psychology, not your or my ability to tell the future. And again, though the pros may do this trade using more complicated derivatives, any amateur can now do the same thing using Exchange Traded Funds.

You Decide by Making Decisions

Some people fail to see the need for an ability to make their own decisions. If there's somebody out there who knows it all already, why not just get some advice from them? Why study, why research, why open a book?

A guy who's been listening to me for years on the radio came up to me at an event and said, "I wanted to thank you for recognizing that there are people who really do want to spend their lives learning." I had another speaking engagement set for that same evening and I was being rushed off, so I just smiled and said thank you. But let me tell you something about people who *say* they want to spend their lives learning.

This may sound a little cynical to you, but I happen to know that everything these people want to know is in the library. Everything they could *ever* want to know about investing and about running their business, it's all right there in the library. There is Valueline, with its terrific stories and updates on thousands of companies you need to know about. There is George Muzea's *Vital Few vs. Trivial Many*; scores of books by Art Laffer. (Just putting yourself near one of the great minds of our century is certain to have an impact on your life); the *American Dream in a Box*, by my bride, Elisea Frishberg; and *Beating the Business Cycle*, by Anirvan Banerji. Every book ever written by my buddy Tobin Smith will make you smarter and richer. I could go on forever, but the point is do you know how many people there are in the public libraries in all of the big cities in the country right now, today?

Remember, everything you'd ever want to know about how to make more money, about the stock market, the economy, your business, about your relationships, everything you could want to know is right there on those shelves! OK? And guess what, in every major city in the United States the public library is *virtually empty*. Because in every one of those cities, I think there are more guys watching Mexican soap operas because they have gorgeous girls with short dresses in them. There are more, wait, let me modify that, there are more people *who don't understand Spanish* watching Mexican soap operas in every major city in the United States than there are at the public library. So let's not kid ourselves.

Why Make Your Own Decisions Anyway?

There are a lot of guys who go on radio or TV for the express purpose of giving stock tips and, of course, rationalizing them. Most of them also have a magic piece of software to sell. For just $19.95, plus shipping and handling of course, it'll show you exactly how he determines these "can't lose" stocks.

All right, I'm being facetious. And all right, yes, I *do* give stock tips on my radio program now and then. I mix them in, because a large part of the audience simply *must* have that, but the truth is I don't really think stock tips are all that valuable. That's why I run my disclaimer every day at the end of my show. It basically says, "Don't go and buy something just because you heard about it here. Get off your butt and do some research of your own."

Sometimes stock tips are just enough to hurt yourself with, much like giving a box cutter to your 10-year-old son to open a box. If he cuts his finger it's because he didn't think ahead. There's no strategy.

He holds down whatever he means to cut and then cuts too close, and there goes the tip of his finger.

Honestly, I think a trip to the library now and then and a little studying can teach you how to make decisions, how to play the game on Wall Street, how to run your business, and how to treat your family—those things are far more important than tips on stocks or anything else. In fact, I believe that I personally could do very well if all I did was buy and sell the Standard and Poor 500 ETF, and maybe just for good measure buy and sell a little gold. I think I could do that without any other options and I could make very good money using nothing more than a little selective timing and the right decision-making.

Einstein said education is what's left if you forget all the facts you learned in school. I think knowledge of the stock market is what's left if you forget everything you know about the stocks and just focus on studying the people. For years my radio program started with my announcer, Sal Monistere, saying, "There's a billionaire inside you..." and that the key to freedom was simply having the right information to work with when the time came for making decisions. That's precisely correct. There *is* someone inside you who often knows exactly what to do.

During the Watergate scandal, I remember watching Richard Nixon make a speech, the one that brought him down. (Hey, I voted for Richard Nixon, and at the time I was rooting for him.) I remember it so well; he was on TV saying, "Your president is not a crook." Suddenly it hit me—the guy is lying! I don't know how I knew it, I just knew it at that moment, and I knew then that he was a goner. Against all odds, that epiphany, that unconscious epiphany was actually correct.

One of my friends, talk-show host Vince Rowe, is a wonderful trader. I know he spent some time in the library at some point, because he's learned how to be a great decision maker. He makes terrific money because he intimately knows a couple of stocks (for example, Starbucks is one of his favorites). He doesn't always buy it—sometimes he sells it—but he knows it so well that he can make money with it almost every day. Vince has learned to trust himself to feel out the relationship between Starbucks stock and the price of the commodity (coffee).

When the commodity price goes up, the anticipated Starbucks profit comes down, and Starbucks stock becomes more volatile when the price of coffee is moving around. Vince Rowe can make money with that knowledge and experience several times a week, and he can catch a move or he can fade a move (going opposite the market), and he can do that and make money in an hour—just because he has the feel of that Starbucks stock. It's his proper timing and expert decision-making ability that keep him on top of the game.

Sometimes, with a little studying, you can just learn a certain gambit and when you see your opening you can take it, and if you're patient enough to wait for your opening you can win with just that one technique. Unfortunately, most people will find a way to lose, even with a great technique or a great stock tip. They'll lose by being overeager, by exiting at the wrong time, by being motivated by a need for self-esteem—all the human weaknesses and foibles that you'll read about throughout this book. Here's the bottom line: It's OK to perk up when you hear a stock tip, but you also have to know how to be a good decision-maker.

Want to take a little survey of yourself and your decision-making? All right then, here goes: You didn't get to pick your kids, but you did get to pick your spouse. How'd that decision work out? You picked your career, how about that? Do good decisions come naturally to you? They can. What does it take to make good decisions?

I've spent a lot of years thinking about this. I've had to because I've made a living playing a game for hundreds of millions of dollars that I just can't afford to lose. I never really wanted to have to rely on my own decisions. But I never could find anyone reliable enough to pin my hopes and my family's future on. I had to learn so I could just do it myself. I even spent a little time in the library. Trust me, nobody's going to do it for you; you have to do it yourself. And by the way, these days you can easily replace the words "in the library" with "at your computer." How much more convenient could it be?

Free That Billionaire Inside You!

Speaking of Starbucks, here's another coffee story. Market research showed you could never sell a $3 cup of coffee to Americans. They'd never buy it. Howard Schultz was living in Milan, sitting at a café, enjoying a cup. He casually had a flash of inspiration and smiled as he thought about it. He figured the idea of people sitting in cafes, leisurely talking and drinking coffee, would also work in the United States. He knew that the price of the coffee—even three or four bucks—wouldn't matter, any more than $7 bar drinks don't matter in the right ambiance. Now, I'd say that was a good decision.

Here's what Howard did, and I'm telling you this because I know you can do it, too. First, he didn't force a decision based on a time schedule. He wasn't compelled to hurry up and come up with a good idea; there was never a hurry. I've shared a few epiphanies with you throughout this book, right? Well, Howard Schultz waited until he had an epiphany. So rule number one is *don't force your decisions.*

Don't feel you have to do something today. I think about that a lot; your money belongs in your pocket unless you have something compelling to do with it. You only take risks when you have a high degree of conviction that you're going to get back much more than you put in. Otherwise you should find a safe way to commit your money, and spend your energy finding bonds that bring the highest return you can get as a lender. I've got a whole section in this book on how to do that.

The next rule to remember is this: When you *do* have that special epiphany, which comes generally when you're not trying to force it, *think it through at least three separate times.* Don't test it out on other people, they tend to either say yes to everything or no to everything; this is *your* epiphany, don't be codependent. Then, think through all the things that can go wrong. In fact, don't just think about them, list them on paper. And as you do this with a clear mind, solutions to these problems and obstacles will come to you. You'll find yourself saying, "If this problem happens I'm gonna sell out. On the other hand, if this happens I'm gonna buy more of this stock, or I'm gonna do more of whatever I did. This is how I'll know." Write it all out.

Here's the next rule: *Don't wait until you feel good about your plan to act*—you're *supposed* to be scared. If you aren't scared, folks, you just don't understand the game. You'd better be scared, not because your plan is wrong, but because the world changes so fast that things can turn against you in the blink of an eye, even when you're right. You don't have to be comfortable. You don't have to feel trust in your decisions. You just learn intellectually to know you have to make decisions.

The more you try to hide behind rules and techniques and research and other people's opinions to simplify your job, the more you're interfering with that billionaire inside you. The most powerful part of you is your unconscious; all you have to do is unblock that billionaire, don't try to force it. You've had these kinds of epiphanies before; you've had them all your life. Think back to what they felt like when you just knew something and you were right, just as I knew that Richard Nixon was lying in that one moment of clarity. Don't commit unless you have that feeling.

Coffee, Tea, or Water?

Maybe you're too late to invest in the concept of coffee on every corner. But let me remind you about one of coffee's chief ingredients (besides the coffee): water. Covering about 71 percent of the Earth's surface, there's a *lot* of water. You don't really get a sense of it until you fly over it for 10 or 20 hours or gaze out at the horizon from the deck of a cruise ship. It's really a *lot* of water. The problem is it's not much good for drinking, irrigation, or anything else we normally associate with the unsalted version. It's pretty amazing to think that less than 2 percent of our usable water is below ground in aquifers or other large gathering pools and pockets. (Seems like all the good stuff we want and need is underground.)

There is no substitute for water. Its daily uses go beyond drinking, sanitation, recreation, and irrigation. Trying to determine all the ways water is used in daily life would be pretty tough. It's a resource like no other, and its value to human life is essential. Now, I know that you know that we've got water problems here on planet Earth. But stop to think about how serious these problems are by considering the following:

- Almost 5,000 children die each day from unsafe water and lack of basic sanitation facilities.
- By 2025, two-thirds of the world's population will be feeling some effect of the global water shortage.
- A lot of the obvious water sources (rivers and lakes) are so polluted that obtaining usable water from them is nearly impossible, and at best extremely difficult.
- Almost 500 million people in some 30 countries currently face severe water shortages.
- Half of the world's population doesn't have proper sanitation.
- Over a billion people don't have clean drinking water.

Most folks agree that the important questions to be asked about water deal with quality, availability, and accessibility. If a company is in the water business, it's considered vital. If it's run well, offers a quality product and service, and has vision for future needs, it can be a very profitable company indeed. Such is the case with Veolia Environment.

Veolia is a French-based diversified company focusing on water, waste management, energy, and transportation. This is truly a global company with more than 336,000 employees and operations on every continent. I'll tell you one of the reasons why I like Veolia, and why it attracted our attention in the first place. It has presence.

Almost one third of the company's business is centered around water. Their website describes the company's goal: "We withdraw water from natural resources and use it to produce and distribute drinking water and industrial water. We then collect and transport wastewater and treat it for reuse or return to the ecosystem. We also take action to preserve water resources before withdrawal, and protect the receiving environment into which wastewater is discharged." They could have said, "Water . . . we do everything." Again, the marketing department gets the kudos—well done, gang.

There are continual changes taking place in the water industry. Veolia's infrastructure spending picked up in late 2009 and 2010, and a lot of that infrastructure spending is going into the water business. Here's a note to be noted: Veolia's shares dropped from nearly $100 in December 2007 to a March 2009 low of $20. Isn't it funny how many more people want to buy the stock at $100 and how few want to touch it at $20?

And before I walk away from Veolia: (And please, stop me if you've heard this one) How do you get Americans to pay more for drinking water than they pay for gasoline? Easy! Just tell 'em it's from France!

More Water

I would be remiss if I didn't include here a discussion about another water company, and this one's *not* in France. Douyuan Global Water Inc. (DGW) is the leading Chinese water filtration and purification company. They operate in three primary categories of products: Circulating Water Treatment Equipment, Water Purification Equipment, and Wastewater Treatment Equipment. The need for their products comes from a combination of rapid industrialization and a lack of drinkable water in China. Demand for clean water in China has tripled in the last 10 years. Some people argue that water will be critical in the growth and modernization of the country—even more so than oil. A market research firm estimated the demand for water treatment products will grow 15.5 percent each year over the next few years.

Even though GE, Siemens, and other multinational companies have similar operations, only DGW offers a direct investment in China's infrastructure and water purification technologies.

Douyuan Global Water was founded in 1992 by Wenhua Guo, and the company just recently went public in the United States in June 2009. It's the only water purification company operating in China that's listed on the NYSE.

The initial price of DGW was around $14. After the first day of trading it closed at more than $21, and (as of this writing) has since jumped to the mid-$30s and stayed in that range. Mr. Guo, the chairman and CEO, still maintains a majority 57 percent of the company. That's a pretty substantial ownership interest by the CEO and a positive sign. According to second-quarter reports, at the end of June 2009 the company had nearly $140 billion in cash—substantially above its total debts and liabilities of less than $17 billion.

Along with an excellent balance sheet, the underlying fundamental story looks very promising. There's a critical need for water purification in China, and the growth rate in China's infrastructure spending looks to be increasing back to pre-global recession levels.

Oh, and remember that little joke I shared with you a few paragraphs back? Well, you can stop laughing now. People around the world, including Americans, are in fact willing to pay more for drinking water (by volume) than they do for gasoline. See? It's not really that funny. This is only going to get worse as time goes on. A lot of the problems in Africa are really over drinking water, and wars are going to be fought over this vital resource over the next decade. If you're interested in investing in this industry, I'd suggest you take a closer look at the two aforementioned companies.

That being said, I want to remind you of something I told you at the very beginning of Chapter One. Don't get confused as we continue to discuss this globalized economy. A major part—let me stress that, a *major* part—of what makes up the world economy is

America and American companies. Our chief trader Karl Eggerss recently did a report on investing in water industry leaders.

That list included Suez SA (SZE) and Veolia Environment, both French companies, along with United Utilities (UU), based in the United Kingdom, but it also featured Ameron International (AMN), a diversified company based in the United States; Danaher Corp (DHR), a leading industrial company that basically provides a lot of the equipment to monitor and test other equipment in the water industry; and finally, Basin Water Inc. (BWTR), a California-based company. Basin is admittedly one of the more speculative picks on the list, however, it probably has the biggest potential.

Check out these companies. There are utility companies and industrial water companies. Some treat the water, some collect the water, some transport the water, and some provide the technology to do all of the above. I encourage you to research these companies and others addressing this global water issue, since the need for solutions is growing. The shortage of usable water is a dismal reality, but the companies working hard to provide answers are also providing excellent opportunities for the prudent investor.

Marine Decision-Making À la Paul Van Riper

Paul Van Riper was a lieutenant general who ran the Marines Leadership and Combat Development School in the '90s. They used the old system of rational analysis: frame the problem, formulate alternatives, collect data, evaluate the options. Every organization teaches the same thing; anything else we'd call irrational. But the general noticed that in real situations—in very tense combat situations—his men kept coming up short. They kept blaming themselves, but they just couldn't make decisions under pressure using this normal business system that all of us think is the right way to make decisions.

After a lot of frustration, after yelling at his men and blaming them for being dense and lazy, the general realized it wasn't the Marines who were no good. Rather, it was the system that was wrong. So the Marine Leadership School went out and found a cognitive psychologist who was studying firemen. Firemen, don't have the time for rational decision-making; they're always on the battlefield, and they just do whatever they think of that might work at that second. They have no time to make a rational analysis. They don't weigh the alternatives; they just do something.

Well, after spending some time with the psychologist, General Van Riper put together his own plan. He brought a group of Marine officers to the New York Mercantile Exchange, because he said the trading pits reminded him of a war room during combat. When they tried trading simulations the Marines got wiped out by the floor traders. No big surprise there; the traders are pros. But a month later, they brought these floor traders to the officers' training base in Quantico, Virginia, to play war games against the Marines. Well, they wiped the Marines out in the war games, too. Now, *that* was a surprise to everybody.

When they analyzed the game, they concluded that the traders were just better gut thinkers. They were practiced at quickly evaluating risks, and they were willing to act decisively on imperfect and contradictory information. Today the Marine Corps official doctrine reads "The intuitive approach is more appropriate for the vast majority of decisions in the fluid, rapidly changing conditions of war, when time and uncertainty are critical factors and creativity is a desirable trait."

Most people think the great chess players like Fischer and Karpov are good because they're thinking 15 moves ahead and that they've got every possible situation well thought out. The fact is that if they were thinking 15 moves ahead and knew the whole chess board, the super computer would be beating the chess champion every time. Nobody can hold as many factors and variables and calculate them as quickly and precisely as a super computer.

But to win at chess, the great chess masters don't think 15 moves ahead. Oh, they do know a lot of gambits from experience. They know a lot of little situations, and they understand perfectly those moves and what's likely to happen, in order. But the great chess champions are champions because they make decisions without tons of information. Remember, they have a timer, and they have to make the decision quickly before the timer turns over.

In fact, the folks who become chess champions are champions because they're able to make the right decisions when there isn't enough time and information for rational decision-making. They just happen to get it right more often than not. Not surprisingly, it turns out that great investors and hedge fund managers turn out to be great chess fans. They're champions of sorts, too, and there are really a lot of similarities in what they do.

Some people just have a feel for making good decisions when there isn't enough information to be rational—they just get it. Joe Montana could just feel where those defensive guys were. He couldn't actually see behind him, but he had a reputation for having eyes in the back of his head because he just knew where those guys were at all times.

George Soros says he gets a backache when he has to change something. He became a billionaire selling pounds short when the British government was stating categorically they would never devalue. Soros borrowed billions in pounds to buy other currencies. In one day he made over a billion dollars when the British currency actually did devalue. Some people are just good at making money decisions.

It isn't the computer program or the method either. Some people just find a way to make money; they use whatever tools are around. The modern tools do make them better, but sometimes you just have to have a feeling, and some people have it more than others. It's not *all* about having the gift, some of it you can learn. You're not gonna be like Joe Montana unless you were born with that gift, but you can learn to be much, much better than the average guy, even under pressure.

After 50 years of experience, I know this is what you have to do. If you can get good at it, terrific; if you can't, face it. Wake up and be in the present, stop thinking so hard. Forget about who thinks what, and don't listen to other people. Stop rehearsing conversations with your parents or anyone else who isn't really there. Stop yearning so hard for the right answer; the world is changing too fast.

I know, you're thinking that if only you could get enough data, enough information, you'd know what to do. This is why people compulsively listen to this boloney about P/E ratios and support levels, analysts' upgrades and downgrades. Most of the time, making money on Wall Street, making money in the stock market, has nothing to do with any of these things—then at different times, it has everything to do with all of them. The point here is you can't rely on any favorite technique except getting as much experience and information into your unconscious and learning to let that beautiful computer inside you do its job.

If you're wide open in the present—if you avoid getting in your own way with fear, greed, wishful thinking—then every once in a while you'll just *get it*. You can feel when that happens, and that's really the only time you should be taking risks. Personally, I don't do anything when I don't have that feeling. And I'll always remember sitting and watching Richard Nixon on TV more than 30 years ago in a little apartment in Greenwich Village and saying to myself, "Hey, wait a minute."

5

Unlock the Billionaire Inside You

Here's the Key, Easy Instructions Included

I n this chapter . . .

- Challenge and opportunity
- Loral Langemeier—she found the cheese
- Some instructional direction—sculpting David
- Seven things about you—write them down
- Basic instincts

Brainpower: Escape from the Herd!

Six billion people—that's how many people you have to compete against, but it's also the number of people there are to buy your stuff. Challenge and opportunity—there's plenty of both to go around. What a great opportunity! Billions of your new neighbors don't have enough of (and could use more of) what you sell. But here's the challenge: Out of those billions of people, the odds are that somebody else—some competitor of yours—sells what you sell. And almost certainly, if you're an American (a member of the richest group who ever lived on Earth), that competitor is willing to work harder and cheaper than you. You only have two ways to win here. You have to be smarter, more courageous, and more ingenious than he is. Or my favorite—the "new" way—you can get paid lots of money for providing that tough competitor the capital he needs, and harness him to work for you.

We Americans have been winning at those kinds of games for a long time, but the more the others learn from us, go to our schools, and pick up our skills, the less chance you have to do it the old way—living from memory. Remember the story, "Who Moved My Cheese?" The whole point of the story is about environmental changes, and the fact that the only way to survive and grow stronger and richer is to use the full capacity of your brain. Memory is easy and comfortable, but it just isn't enough.

Until now, you may have gotten away with simply jumping from one bandwagon to another, following some tip or article leading to another way of scoring some easy profits. When enough money is flowing around, almost anything works. It's easy to confuse low interest rates and lack of competition with genius. This belief in the easy answer really misses the point, and rarely ends well.

Most technology investors had a wonderful run back in the '90s. To borrow from basketball, the offense was working. But they totally forgot that boring old defense, and those investors lost back most or all of their stock market profits when the competition got a little tougher. Like the lemmings, they didn't wake up until they were already over the cliff.

I've been talking about this in a hundred different ways for years. For example, I wrote this thought into a radio script in the summer of 2008. I said then that many real estate house flippers were in the process of doing the same thing as the tech lemmings. They jumped on a popular bandwagon after everybody already knew about it, and I predicted they would also end up with nothing.

So here, my sadder and wiser countrymen, is what you have to get. You have to understand it fully—you have to own it—because it is the key to lasting success in everything you do that involves human beings. The best analogy I can think of is this: Looking back on the painful bust of the tech stocks, I asked the real estate lemmings to consider what had happened to their cousins, the tech lemmings. "How can you possibly expect the world to pay you a lot of money, or heap any kind of fabulous rewards on you for jumping on a bandwagon and putting money into tech stocks, when those companies already had all the money they needed?"

All those tech investor lemmings were doing was trading paper among themselves. All the money had been raised to enable those tech companies to do business long before. The lemmings were simply pouring money into the secondary market and pushing up the price of the paper. All of that trading money was floating around, but none of it was going to the companies whose stocks were being traded. (You may want to go back a few chapters and reread the little story about the black velvet paintings.)

So, in the next round, at the time of the house-buying-lemming-monologue, investors just scurried around paying top dollar for houses. Enough houses were already built. The baby boomers were aging, to be replaced by a much smaller generation. There was zero social utility in extending that house industry boom. The investors were clearly not making anything happen, so why would they expect society to reward them for simply following the crowd?

How many 'real estate investors' did any kind of real reflection on demographics, future demand for homes, historical real estate price trends, or anything else that an awakened investor would consider? Do you know any?

Those homebuyers at the peak of the market were just gambling with time. They were investing in the opening of the hundred millionth house-flipping business. To do that, they learned the most superficial way to value homes. They learned how to buy the homes wholesale without any real understanding of supply and demand, with no real thought about changing demographics. They brought those homes to market, not as homes but as some kind of bargaining chip—like baseball cards—just as the late-to-the-party tech investors had done before them. In fact, many of them were the late-to-the-party tech investors, repeating the same habit. That's just what lemmings do! They expected to get paid basically for being distributors of bargaining chips.

That kind of lemming-like activity is not, and never really was, an investment. They were just buying themselves a hard, risky job. I guess for a ditch digger, that activity felt like a step up, at least for a while. But these weren't just ditch-diggers. They were also doctors. They were college professors and engineers. They found out that their jobs were really much better. Why? Because they were actually spending their lives helping people get what they want. They were selling scarce skills that made a difference, and justifiably they received the rewards of society, in a pretty enduring way.

As Investor 2.0, you are awake. You're clear that by investing we mean that *you* don't work—your *money* works and your *brain* works so you don't have to. You're always conscious that the world is ready and willing to pay you well for the use of your capital, when you use it to do something valuable that helps people get what they want. You know you'll be paid a lot when you're extra resourceful, extra brave, or extra early because you added something special to the mix of humanity.

Throughout this book I'm sharing with you not only my ideas, but the fabulous ideas of the smartest, most successful investors, traders, and entrepreneurs on Earth. My special gift from God is that I have the good fortune to spend my life surrounded by these brilliant and inspiring people. Most people get to see them for two minutes here and two minutes there. I spend hours with them every day. It rubs off, too. It has made me far more financially comfortable and independent than I ever expected to be, and I am blessed with the wonderful opportunity of getting to share what I learn with you.

A *Real* "Real Estate Lady"—The Loral Langemeier Story

Right here, I have to tell you about one of the smartest and coolest ladies I know, the very famous and successful Loral Langemeier. Loral saw the real estate market, exactly as I've been describing to you, but she thinks just the way you're learning to think. Loral is truly Investor 2.0, maybe I'd call her investor 3.0, because I don't know anybody like her right now.

Loral saw the carnage in the real estate market. She saw all the lemmings that had been looking for easy money in a place where everybody already was. When the real estate market crashed all over the country, the instinctive thing to do would be to seek parts of the country that are holding up the best, where there had been no real appreciation, so there was nothing to crash.

Loral realized that the real estate bust was worst in the places that are most beautiful, most entertaining—the place people really want to be! She saw the banks getting stuck with hundreds of homes in places like Las Vegas and other highly desirable locations around the country.

She saw homes—hundreds of them—that were built to be sold for $250,000 and on the market for $150,000. And the banks were stuck with them. So she and her people did a careful analysis of all the homes the banks were stuck with, and also thoroughly analyzed the banks themselves. Then she went to those banks that were stuck the most, and that were the most vulnerable, and said to them, "Look, this is costing you a fortune, and it's going to put your company out of business and maybe cost you your job. How about I take all 150 homes off your hands for 80 grand apiece? You'll be out of trouble, the homes will be absorbed by people who can now afford to live in them, the neighborhoods won't be blighted, life will go on, and everybody wins." Loral and her students and followers deserve to become rich as they help people get what they want. And in the course of it all, they're becoming rich.

This is how Investor 2.0 works. Take it from me: Working smart is a lot more fun and much more lucrative than working hard. Investor 2.0 rejoices in the knowledge and deep understanding that this level of ingenuity, responsibility, and courage is scarce. The beauty of putting all this into practice is that you become rich and then you attract the money you deserve as you join with other awakened investors around the world to build the most productive society that has ever existed.

The most profitable question in the English language is "How can I use my capital to help people get what they want? What's the best way for me to help more people get what they really want—not just what they say they want!" By the way, the least profitable words in the English language are "Where has this been all my life?" That's the question asked by novices who have just been turned on to some new trading software or idea, about which they know very little, right after they have made some quick, easy money on the idea. The more insightful, ingenious, courageous, and determined you are as you go about this, the more successful you will be at helping more people get what they want. The earlier you get to it, the more you will be rewarded.

Exercise—Chip Away Until You See David

We do a lot of talking about money and investments. I know I do, it's my business, but I can't open a paper or magazine or turn on the TV or radio without seeing or hearing some commentary about the condition of things: The economy does this, the market does that, this chart shows how they correlate, and the government plays a role in all of it! Does any of this really determine your success or failure? Not at all. What determines your success is you.

Conditions come and go, but the few winners just continue to find a way to win. And the habitual losers always find a way to lose. I've compared notes with many of the most famous and successful people in a lot of different walks of life, not just investing. We start every day and every decision with a clear focus on what we want to accomplish, and we define our goals. Most of the time people don't know, and they don't even know that they don't know. So before we go another moment let me challenge you to identify your investment goals for today. If you don't know, you've got to work on that first.

Don't be fooled into thinking that success in your financial life is about stock tips. I advise you to stay out of investing until you have a clear picture of how investments fit into your life today. The first thing to do is work on what it is you're trying to accomplish. And if you're not sure exactly what your goals are and what results you are trying to create, one of the best ways to find out is the technique we're going to use right now.

Let's start by making a list of seven things about you and your life that are consistent with what you're trying to create for yourself. Take your time. If you can't think of seven things that are consistent with what you want in your life, lower the importance level a little bit— just make sure you do seven of them. We're talking about things that are actually results that you have created, and every result in your life is something that you have created.

Next you're going to put seven more numbers down, and list seven things that are *not* consistent with what you want in your life. Be clear on this part; list what is going on that is *not* consistent with what you want in your life. Just start chipping away as Michelangelo did. Remember, he made a great sculpture of David by taking a large block of marble and chipping away everything that didn't look like David. So let's make a great life by chipping away those things that you don't want.

Take your time and do this properly. You'll see that the ease with which you find things that are *not* consistent with what you want will give you a pretty good idea of what your state of mind is. When you're pretty depressed, all you can think of is things you don't like. When you're feeling really good, all you can think of is things that you like. With this little exercise, we're simply forcing ourselves to think of seven of each.

Now we're going to take that list of seven results that you created that are not consistent with what you want in your life, and you're going to write down the antonym, the *opposite* of what you don't want. For example, if I said, *I am overweight; it is not consistent with what I want.* The antonym for that would be *I look fabulous, and I'm in total control of my weight.*

Go through all seven of the things that are in your life that you don't want and write down the seven opposites. The fact of the matter is that if you just accomplish those seven goals, your life will be much better. If you just make those seven changes in your life, your life will be far better. This gives you something to focus on. You don't have to be on anybody else's agenda, you can simply focus on these things.

What I like to do is to read the results I intend to create. I read them every morning and every night, and I get them absolutely, indelibly marked on my brain. And the more I do it, the easier it is to commit myself to doing these things. Using this simple technique, I've been able to create everything in my life as a reality that I have ever managed to get into my brain.

I've talked with some of the most successful people in the world. I can tell you for certain that every one of them who has been able to create and sustain unbelievable success has learned the secret that I've just told you. They do it, they stick with it, they practice it, and they know that it works. I'm not asking you to believe anything; you can't really believe something until you do it. And you'll find that you can't control what you believe, but you *can* control what you do.

More David-Chiseling

Let me give you some suggestions about some of the things to chip away, things that don't "look like David." Chip away risking your hard-earned savings without a clear intense belief that what you're doing is profitable; don't ever do that again. Take risks only when you are being overpaid. Be like an insurance company, make sure that you are being overpaid for the risks you take. Make a clear assessment of the impact on your life of winning and losing.

A lot of people took risks because they were running on ego, because they wanted to be the smartest guy at the golf course, because they were rehearsing in their mind the fun of telling somebody how smart they were. They had everything they wanted and little chance of really improving their lifestyle, but a big loss would have a profound effect on them. To satisfy their emotional desire for respect and self-esteem, they risked their money and their lifestyle.

Ask yourself how much ego plays in your investment decisions. How much does the desire to think of yourself as smart affect the decisions you make? How much does that desire make you reluctant to sell at the right time when it turns out that you are wrong? For example, are you prone to holding on because the pain of losing is too great? You shouldn't really feel bad about this tendency; we all have it, that's how humans are. In fact, we've had this tendency for eons. We were doing this long before we even learned how to talk to each other. It's just another one of those "cavemen don't get rich" stories.

And speaking of stories, I've got one for you I promise you're gonna love. It's about monkeys. Just go with me on this one, OK? Every day this guy brings bananas in during a psychological test of these two groups of monkeys. In the first group, on the first day, he comes in with a banana for each monkey. He does this for a time, and he's got some happy monkeys. Then after a while he starts to bring in two bananas for each. The monkeys have become accustomed to getting one banana, so they're surprised, but they're not asking any questions. They're loving *this* guy, right?

Now, with the other group of monkeys the guy brings in two bananas every day right from the start. And that group's pretty content, too. No problem. Well, after a time, he cuts that group down to one banana. Of course, the monkeys go nuts: "Where's my other banana, meathead?" They absolutely begin to loathe this guy. He's showing up with a banana, and they're furious with him—they hate the guy. Now over time, each group got the same number of bananas. But with the first group where they expected one and eventually were surprised by two, they loved him and were very happy; in the second group, well, you get it I'm sure. But look what we've learned.

This experiment shows just how unbalanced the fear of loss is versus the desire for gain. Obviously for a man trying to survive as an animal in the wild, losing (meaning getting killed and eaten) was something that he couldn't really afford. You lose and get eaten one time, and that's it! You and I are hardwired to be willing to give up many wins to avoid one loss. Now while that makes sense to a caveman, it's a losing proposition on Wall Street, where winning and losing are each worth the same number of points. The bias does not save your life anymore, but it costs you cold, hard cash. You're competing against seasoned pros on Wall Street. You're competing against people who have none of the weaknesses we're talking about.

If some of these seasoned people have any weaknesses at all, they know about them. They've worked on them, they've mastered them, and they have information and resources you don't have. You meet a lot of these guys on my radio program. If you're weak these people are going to take your money, and *then* they're going to eat your lunch. They love sharing the information they have with you, but they will take your money *in a minute*. So how can you compete against very strong adversaries? Obviously many of the people who are reading this book just can't compete in some areas; they don't have the equipment. I hope you've decided you're not one of them.

A guy came up to me at a seminar I did last week and he seemed like a very nice guy and asked about gold futures. Somehow somebody who sells gold futures got his name, or found him randomly, or he's invested in things like that before, and is on their list—I don't know how they got him. Anyway, a very tough sales guy is now repeatedly calling him, and you've heard the story they tell him: $5,000 will control $100,000 worth of gold, and the dollar is going to be bad, and the economy is going to be bad, and inflation is coming, and all of that stuff.

So the guy asks me, "Is gold looking good? Should I invest with this guy that's been calling me from Florida?" I said, "Well, yeah, gold looks OK. Should you invest? I don't know. What do you know about options or futures? And what do you know about gold? And why do you want to invest in futures?" He says, "Because there's so much leverage—$5,000 will control $100,000" and blah, blah, blah. So I asked him, "Why is that good? Can you afford $100,000 speculation on gold? Do you know enough about gold to invest $100,000 in it?" He says, "Well, hey, but it's only $5,000."

No, it's a $100,000 investment in futures with a $5,000 deposit. It moves like $100,000. If you think of it as a $5,000 investment, you're going to get cleaned out right away. You have to be willing to accept a $20,000 fluctuation on $100,000 worth of a commodity. A 20 percent move in an extreme case is not a big deal. You can't afford to get that kind of money into this one investment. I've explained this to the guy, and he says, "Why, is it because the commission is too high?" No, not the commission, the commission doesn't matter at all, that's just one little thing that's stacked against you. The question is do you have a firm conviction that you want a $100,000 worth of gold?

See, he thinks his friend (the high pressure salesman) is going to help and guide him. And if this was you, I think you ought to ask this friend a couple of questions. Like for instance, if you know when to buy and sell gold, shouldn't you have a lot of money? Here's another question: Do rich people spend their lives and their time calling up strangers in other states to offer them advice on investments? Am I crazy or are these pretty easy questions with readily apparent answers? Help me out here.

I mean what could possibly be in your mind as you meander along to the slaughter; what could you be thinking? What is the lamb thinking as he's being lured along at the slaughterhouse? "*Oh, what a nice man, he wants me to go in that nice room. Hmm, smells like other lambs in there. I wonder what they're doing.*" That may very well be what the lamb is saying; whaddya think?

You don't have to be an expert on everything. If you have a plan and a clear image of what you're doing, you only have to be good at a few things. And if you get very good at a few things, you should stick to them. You can be as good as anybody alive if you'll get good at a few things and stick to them. Immediately somebody is going to come and say, "*Okay, here's another idea, this is great! And everybody is getting rich on it . . .*", and you're going to be tempted to follow along.

Then you're going to think of this book and you're going to remember the guy who sets his own agenda in his life and his investments. He's the guy who sticks with his own game plan. And you'll remember that you're a part of the union of people who use their brains to get a better deal, and you'll either say, "*Forget it*" or you'll say, "*I want to know more about it. I'm gonna become one of the world's foremost authorities on that one thing. I know I can do this. Send me everything you've got on it, and I'll start my research.*" And then folks, do what Ronald Reagan always did: trust. But always, *always* cut the cards.

The Death of Investor 1.0

Almost everybody in the United States is mentally stuck in the 1990s. Tens of millions of Americans are waiting for the resumption of our financial leadership, dominance, and economic growth. In fact, they're betting everything on it. We're talking countless trillions of dollars. This is money people have been counting on to keep them comfortable when they're too old to work, money they're planning to use to educate their children and grandchildren, money they hope to use to start or build a business.

They think they're being conservative and prudent, but the life savings they've invested in companies, funds, and assets are really just bets on the normally powerful growth of the U.S. economy. It sounds like a good bet, right? They're making it because it's always worked—or so they think! The bet produced timely results in the '80s and '90s, and for Investor 1.0, that means it always has and it always will.

But the bet has not always worked for people who need results within 10 or 20 years. Frankly, my work shows the United States recovering a little for the near future, which will feel pretty good, but then I see our economy and stock market stagnating for a long, long time—maybe the rest of my life. So, if you're an amateur, you're asking yourself, "Is Dan right about this?" And that is exactly the wrong question. You aren't going to make yourself rich by seeking a fortune teller. If you or I could really tell the future, don't you think we'd both be trillionaires by now?

The real questions you should be asking—the questions Investor 2.0 asks—are these:

- What are the chances that some other countries, whose leaders were educated in the best U.S. universities, will change their rules to be more business friendly and attract the capital and resources that used to flow into the United States 10 years ago? Fifty-fifty maybe?
- What about taxing risk-takers and rewarding poorly performing, less efficient businesses? What are the chances that those policies could contribute to some stagnation? Fifty-fifty?
- What are the chances that the decisions our country is making right now, combined with the aging baby-boom population, will limit growth in the United States? Fifty-fifty, do you think?
- And what about the fact that baby boomers, who were the engine of progress for the past generation, are getting older and considering moving themselves out to pasture? Does it matter that the baby boomers are now being replaced by a much smaller and less hungry population of their children, while other countries are now demonstrating the courage, creativity, and ingenuity that we showed when we were hungry? What are the chances of this demographic change impacting growth in the U.S. economy, compared to other economies over the next decade? Fifty-fifty?

So now let me ask you this: Are you in the habit of calculating the risks and likely rewards when you bet your life savings on something, or do you think you should just act on some easy combination of habit, emotion, wishful thinking, and impulse? If you take the mindless route, it is because you are (or up to now you have been), Investor 1.0. It's time for a change.

Most Americans Aren't Hedging at All

Short-term traders, long-term investors, beginners, supposed experts—most are mindlessly betting on a resumption of the '90s. Frankly, the bet has very low odds of winning, but most Americans aren't hedging that bet at all. They're doing nothing to provide themselves a margin of safety in a very iffy situation, because they really aren't thinking. They're remembering. They aren't really in love with the investments they now hold. They're in love with what those investments *used* to be, and they're betting everything.

Investor 2.0 is a new species on the rise, replacing the more primitive, less advanced Investor 1.0. It's much the same thing that happened when Homo sapiens replaced Neanderthal man. Investor 2.0 always keeps in mind the basic truth that any clear thinking, experienced, and successful bettor lives by this one rule: No matter how many times you win, if you continue to let everything ride, you end up broke, because once you lose, you're all the way back to square one.

And this mistake will have a devastating impact, because most American baby boomers—at least the ones I know—no longer have the grit to start over. If forced by dire circumstances, I'm fully confident their children will do whatever it takes to recover past glory, but I think there is a good chance the parents just aren't ready, and it is the parents who are in charge right now. This is the irony of Investor 1.0. Like the Neanderthal 30,000 years ago, Investor 1.0 has just about all the tools he needs and all the necessary innate brain power. Neanderthal man just never had the epiphany that would help him survive, prosper, and inherit the earth.

While we're on the subject, scientists have been puzzling for decades about why Homo sapiens just simply replaced Neanderthal. At first, the theory was that Neanderthal didn't have the brain capacity, but later we found that his brain was in fact physically equal to ours. Then researchers thought he didn't have the right musculature or bone structure in the mouth, tongue, or throat to talk well. Wrong again.

Then, they discovered that a disproportionate number of Neanderthals were found to have broken bones in their legs and arms. Finally! Neanderthal was equal to modern humans in every way, but his bones were brittle! That explained it, right? But Neanderthal's bones turned out to be just as dense and just as strong as ours. His bones were *not* more prone to breakage. Well, guess what? Finally—*finally*—we have the answer to this puzzle. Here's why we survived and replaced Neanderthal man as the dominant species on the planet:

Some human, around 30,000 years ago realized that you could throw your spear and kill your prey (or your enemy) from a distance. Our early ancestors started to design weapons for hunting and for war that could be *thrown*. Neanderthal continued to do all his hunting and fighting the same way he always had. He built his spears and axes for hitting and thrusting, *not* for throwing.

And of course, he frequently broke his arms, his legs, and his skull because he did all his fighting and hunting hand-to-hand. We (humans) not only designed our spears and axes as projectiles, but this cultural change also combined with natural selection to encourage the survival of humans with shoulders that were better for throwing. Human 2.0 woke up and adapted. Human 1.0 just kept doing things the way he always had.

Technology has forever changed our society. By making information much easier to share, and by enhancing communication a hundred-thousand-fold, human potential has been enhanced a million-fold. As competition has stiffened with six billion players, instead of a couple of hundred million, so opportunity has exploded. If you are competing with billions of humans, you can be sure some of them are awake, conscious, and using their brains. In this new environment, you will not be able to win by relying on your memory.

Investor 1.0 versus Investor 2.0

To simplify life in a complex world, it makes sense to apply past learning, to follow the lead of smarter and more experienced leaders, to remember how things have worked in the past, and to rely on those memories. For several billion years, our Earth has been in a state of constant change, but for the most part, those changes came very slowly by today's standards.

In 1980, hardly anyone trusted the stock market as a way to save for retirement. That's because we had lived through two decades of gross mismanagement of the country and the economy. President Nixon tried price controls, and they didn't work. (We'll get into more detail on these times later in the book, when the facts help illuminate important points.)

For now, it's enough to remember that our country lost stature, our currency fell in value, and gold ran up to unprecedented heights. In real terms (adjusted for inflation), stocks lost 70 percent of their value between the mid-1960s and the early 1980s. So when people wanted to save assets to provide for their security or retirement, they just didn't think of the stock market as a viable tool.

People kept their savings in bank accounts, life insurance policies, and real estate. At that time, inflation had been kind to real estate values, and people believed that real estate was a safe place to keep money. Real estate would always appreciate because, as the old saying goes, "They aren't making any more of it."

Instincts and Impulses

There are a variety of impulsive human behaviors—some good, some not so good. Let's see if we can identify them and how they affect your everyday life, as well as your life as an investor. Some of them are repetitive and, more importantly, counter-productive. Here's one that came about and was probably very useful—for a caveman. (Unfortunately, as you'll soon see, it's not very useful today on Wall Street.)

Take a look at a 100-year market chart. In 1980, folks didn't think they could make any money in stocks because that market was way too risky. They were only comfortable putting their money in a good safe bank. The folks who did that during the 1970s caught a nice big fat round of inflation, and it cost them as much or more than anybody had ever lost in the stock market. Their purchasing power went down; it just happened to them because they defined something as safe. Why? Because it had been working for the past 20 years.

Now look at the next 20-year period starting at 1980. The stock market goes up, and there's seemingly endless productivity. Your impulse is to expect it to continue. Around the year 2000, at the very moment when people expected that the stock market was an easy ride, when it was expected to continue rising, that was the precise spot where it stopped going up.

And in fact, so far, we can say it's held true to form for the next 10 years. The impulse is to extrapolate and believe that whatever is happening now is going to continue. But that's the exact opposite of what's true. We live in a cyclical world where things keep coming back around. For example the cure for high prices is higher prices. When they get too high, people shun those products that are priced too high, they find some alternate, and lo and behold, the prices start coming down.

In 1980 nobody was willing to buy stocks, because stocks had failed to produce easy profits for almost two decades. The banks looked pretty good, but inflation killed the value of the dollar. That left real estate. Ah yes, real estate, the darling of the investment world. Until 1985 that is, when real estate prices had escalated so much that they became, well, overpriced. So much so that even the secured lenders (the banks) were victimized, and many of them failed because of it. Real estate prices came down, and the cycle was setting up to begin again. Sure, you want to get in at the right part of the cycle. The impulse—and this is the part that can be costly—is to be so anxious that you've got to get in, get out, or do something, anything, *right now*. If it lasts 20 years, it feels to humans like forever; it's a glaring weakness that would allow a species with a longer life to defeat us, even if we were as smart and strong as they were.

In addition to this nutty tendency to assume everything will stay the same as today, we have another tendency that worked great 500,000 years ago, and is a money-loser on Wall Street in the 21st century. We are genetically hard-wired to do things in the exact opposite manner of what's best for us as financial beings in year 2009. Why? Because we still have these instincts that evolved in our species long ago. What we really want is to be slender and handsome and svelte and gorgeous and healthy with low cholesterol. We also want to accumulate more things. And finally, we want to be important in our group and have high status. The higher-status animals in a species are usually higher on the list to survive, procreate, and pass on their genes.

But our instincts lead us to produce the exact opposite results, because although we want to be slim and trim and eat sparingly, you still have to face this reality: If you compare this slim and trim representative of the species to the one that sits in his cave gorging himself, storing fat for the long, cold winter ahead, which do you think would survive? Sure, the fat guy. (He can always exercise *next* summer, right?)

We also want to have lots of things, too. But in today's world, we have homes and mini-storage to keep them in, we have trucks to transport them; those poor ancestors had no refrigerators even, so the survivors were the ones who would naturally eat and consume everything in sight with no plans for later whatsoever. Thus another instinct is developed that is counter to what is sensible. Trim is sensible. Your counter-instinct is to be fat and compulsively use up all your resources the minute you get your hands on them.

By the way, saving energy was another important survival trait. That's why we find it so difficult to get ourselves to exercise regularly. As I said before, we are genetically bred to do the opposite of what is best for us as investors. This is simply a story about why you have to do exactly the opposite of what your instincts tell you. It may sound strange, but when you have an impulse to follow your instinct, it's usually wrong.

So here we find ourselves, a product of the last great trend. Many Americans learned most of what they now believe about investing, growing their money, and interfacing with the economy during the years from 1980 to 2000. In 1980, hardly anyone was willing to put important savings into the stock market. Interest rates were at 15 percent, inflation was astronomical, and stock values had been falling in real terms since the 1960s. Three horrible presidents in a row combined with very poor public policy to create an environment where the public lost confidence in paper assets and our institutions' ability to fulfill promises.

In repairing the economy and the confidence of the public, Ronald Reagan, along with my partner Dr. Art Laffer, put into place a 20-year period of falling interest rates, rising confidence, a spirit of innovation, and a new willingness to assume risk that carried our country to a dominant position unchallenged by anyone on the planet. Over those 20 years, stocks simply went up! If you owned them you got richer. You really didn't need special techniques or special silver bullets, but since wonderful conditions are easily confused with genius, you were treated to an avalanche of new techniques. And the truth is if you add the period from 1980 to 2000 on to any study, you can prove that virtually any system or idea works.

Those were the days, my friends, the days of the "Dogs of the Dow," the theory that says you should buy the worst stocks in the

Dow Industrials every year. Then there's the theory that suggests you should invest or sell stock in $50 billion-dollar companies based on to-the-penny predictions made by employees of companies who get paid for selling you stocks, and based on the expectation of pinpoint accuracy in predicting earnings. No matter that we all know those analysts can't even tell you what their wives will spend at the mall this coming weekend! And as you know, there are thousands of other ideas just as crazy, and millions who believe in them, even though none of these ideas have worked in more than eight years. The truth is the ideas never worked, but the great conditions deceived many.

In the 1980s and 1990s, everything seemed to work, because none of that stuff was necessary. Stock prices just went up—almost all of them. By contrast, no matter what silver bullet they believe in, most of today's investors have failed to make money this month, this year, or this decade. The fact is that many of us (you, not me) still believe in silver bullets and magic formulas—I'll explain why later—but those who keep relying on these kinds of tools simply aren't getting richer, even though the world economy has grown faster in the past decade than it ever has in history.

If He Could Just Buy One Stock . . .

Before we move on I want to share an idea with you. It's something I got from my good friend Tobin Smith, one of the best guys alive at spotting societal change and cashing in on it. Toby came back from a trip to China, came on my show, and said, "Dan, if I could only buy one stock and put it away for 10 years, this would be the one."

He was talking about ChinaTel Group, Inc (CHTL.OB). Now before I go a step farther, let me say what you know I'm going to say: There's a gamble here. Toby said *he* might be willing to buy it. He didn't say *you* should buy it. I'm not suggesting you buy it either, OK? If fact, I can't actually even think about buying this as part of my day job; it's just too small and illiquid. But as an individual? Hey, to sock away a little of this stock in a drawer (maybe your *sock* drawer) and then look at it again in a couple of years could be fun. (I actually bought it for my 11-year-old son for his birthday.)

ChinaTel Group, Inc. was formed through the merger of Truss-net USA and 49 percent of Chinacomm Ltd. on May 21, 2008. The company's main business is the engineering and consulting service to build a 3.5 GHz wireless broadband telecommunications network in China. CHTL was given the exclusive license to build and operate a WiMAX network in 29 cities by the Chinese government. The licensing is valid until February 2013, and it includes major cities like Beijing, Shanghai, and Guangzhou.

This is the kind of monopoly that created the big winners of the 1990s, and they could make some adventurous investors very, very rich. On the other hand, the company doesn't have a lot of stock outstanding, and it could be very difficult to sell if something bad happened—you could spend all day writing down dozens of things that *could* go wrong.

One other note, just for good measure: Through the acquisition of 95 percent of Perusat, S.A., which has exclusive licenses for WiMAX through most of Peru, ChinaTel Group now plans to run the network not only in China, but in Peru as well as the rest of Latin America.

6

Being Investor 2.0

Replace Your Old-World View

I n this chapter . . .

- In a minute, Ozzie & Harriet, but first, "Alibaba!"
- Is $250,000 per year enough?
- Creating results
- Erase your old worldview, embrace the world without borders
- In the studio—Frank Cappiello

"Global Trade Starts Here"

Do you feel yourself evolving? Is your brain adapting to this new borderless world of opportunities?

OK, so this morning, you'd like to buy something made in China? That's easy—just walk down any aisle at Wal-Mart and you're inundated with that stuff. But what if you'd like to buy a couple of hundred thousand pieces? How do you buy direct from China? Or maybe Bulgaria?

The answer is a company called Alibaba or, more to the point, Alibaba.com. You simply specify what you want and where you want to buy it from, and—bingo—Alibaba makes the deal happen. It's amazing to just watch the deals go by. They handle everything imaginable. Dice made in Bulgaria. How about an E-bike that runs on a lithium battery? No problem, minimum order 100. It's all wholesale, not retail. All business to business, Alibaba.com matches suppliers with wholesalers.

You need some folding paper binoculars with plastic lenses? Alibaba will hook you up with Joyful Manufacturing (sounds like a fun company). Again, your minimum order would have to be around 20,000 pieces, but if you've got a hot market, they can supply you with up to 300,000 pieces per month. Pretty cool, right? Even frozen fish bait is available, as long as you can accept a minimum of 25 metric tons. I know, that's a lot. But imagine the fish you could catch!

The slogan on their webpage is "Global trade starts here." If Baidu is the Google of China, then Alibaba is the e-Bay or the Amazon. Taobao.com (the Alibaba brand in China) accounts for 2 percent of China's retail sales.

We got to talking about this company on the radio not long ago, and were discussing the idea that Alibaba is really a meeting place for buyers and sellers. I wasn't pushing the conversation in this direction, but apparently I'd set the stage for a discussion about the e-Bay concept. First I got a few callers who wondered if their latest idea, invention, whatever might be a good candidate for sales via Alibaba. Before you know it, I had some of the folks from around the studio sticking their heads in, listening intently. It seems like everybody's got a "next big thing" idea floating around in their heads.

The answer is a resounding "Yes." This is the sort of place that attracts great ideas and great thinkers. In fact, you don't even need to be an inventor of new products. If a fellow had a mind to, he could literally buy from any number of the suppliers available through Alibaba. And in the right quantities, prices are so incredibly low that the profits at resale are unimaginable. This is the kind of excitement generated by forward-thinking companies. Alibaba is one of them, and its growth potential certainly makes this a viable investment for some people.

The company intends to boost exports from small to medium Chinese companies. They match Chinese suppliers with corporate buyers around the world. They are willing to sacrifice short-term profits to become a global brand. Their goal of zero profit means they'll put everything into growth. (They cut subscriber fees by 60 percent to sign up more subscribers.) Yahoo owns roughly 40 percent, company founder Jerry Yang is on the board, and Cisco is also a big investor. They also have a partnership with FedEx; they'll ship at a discount if you buy on Alibaba.

Here are some numbers: 2009 first quarter revenue of $118 million, up 19 percent. (Second quarter profit fell 34 percent, but revenue rose 24 percent.) At the time of this writing, paid members had risen 44 percent to about 500,000. There were roughly 2 million registered users in the United States and growing, with over 32 million registered on the Chinese language site. They had just started a $30 million ad campaign, targeting small business owners. The campaign features success stories of entrepreneurs who made it big by sourcing materials through Alibaba.com. The slogan is "Find it. Make it. Sell it."

Who knows when you're reading this? Maybe it's 2030 and you've found this book behind your grandfather's chest of drawers. But I'm writing it mostly during 2009–2010, and as of today, Alibaba pink sheets, trades 15,000 to 20,000 shares a day. On Friday, November 27th, the day after Thanksgiving 2009, it closed at $2.27 and traded 15,500 shares.

Maybe it's not 2030 yet. Maybe you were one of the first to pick up a copy of this book. That being the case, as far as Alibaba is concerned, you're probably still early, this is going to take patience. And a final note on this one: Use caution. The founder said that shareholders were not his top priority.

Investor 2.0—Destined for Riches (*You are awake, now look around*)

Equity investors place their bets on growth of sales and profits. But today, our society's policies are totally aimed at how the pie is divided, instead of focusing on growing the pie. Those who would contribute to growing the pie are considered the enemy. Taking risk in search of reward is considered greed, with no consciousness that personal desire for acquisition is what has powered the development of the greatest wealth-building machine ever created by man. Fiscal policy aimed at encouraging entitlement and taxing risk-taking will not grow the pie.

For example, innovation and invention can occur anywhere. They're not unique to any one social group. But let's be realistic. How many new inventions are developed and brought to market by people who make less than $250,000 per year? How many new jobs will be created by people who make less than $250,000 per year? The answer in both cases is very few. And the way we currently handle the problem is to take from the risk takers, and look to government to take up the slack. Yet, government doesn't make decisions based on economics or efficiency. Government makes ideological value judgments. I assure you that you would be shocked if you multiply this inefficiency by 300 million people, reduce available capital by the interest payments on trillions of dollars of debt, and then calculate how much less our country will invent and produce over the next several years.

If the villains are greedy capitalists, the heroes are "The Nelsons"—Ozzie, Harriet, David, and Ricky. They were indeed the salt of the earth, and they lived in a less complex economy. But before you decide that's where you want to go, remember this: They lived in a 1,500-square-foot house with one bathroom and a one car garage (with *one* car in it). They didn't all have separate phone numbers and a high-definition TV for each member of the family. They didn't have an extra refrigerator in the laundry room to store their Nutri-System. The clearer this becomes to the market, the more U.S. lifestyles will be adjusted downward toward Nelson levels.

So here we are: the "union of people who use our brains" to get a better deal, and the environment we're headed into isn't the one we've been in for most of our adult lives. That means we won't be able to survive if, as I've stated before, we continue to try to live on memory, so this is going to be a classic exercise in dynamic creation.

Dynamic creation is my short term for how I choose to live my life. It's based on a very simple idea. A successful adapter is someone who is able to change his or her worldview, when the facts change. Sounds like something we'd all want to do, right?

Sure, but it takes a lot of energy. We enjoy living on memory; it's easier. You see, we emerged as human beings at a time when changes generally occurred over thousands (or hundreds of thousands) of years. Another characteristic that's hardwired into us is a tendency to love stability and resent change. It's an animal instinct to feel safer with a home-field advantage, and that translates into being familiar with the environment. That's how we want things to be: stable, unchanged, familiar. But in 2009, it's just simply not the way things are.

So, wake up! Once you're in the mood and you've embraced our exciting, stimulating, full-of-opportunity, rapidly changing environment, you'll find it exhilarating and gratifying to adeptly deal with it, especially when you're way ahead of the millions of Americans who just haven't caught on to what's happening. That's exactly what you're going to have to do in order to have the life you want today. We've created this world; let's be part of the few Americans who embrace and enjoy it!

I know what you're thinking. That I make it sound easy. I certainly don't mean to make it sound easy. Nothing worth gaining is ever easy. But I can help you, by showing you a few steps you have to take to achieve the goal I've laid out for you. Easy? No. Do-able? Of course. Pay attention, and I'll show you how, step by step.

The steps:

- Understand the real facts as well as possible.
- Erase your current worldview.
- Get clear on your new worldview, based on today's facts.
- Focus on the results you choose to create.
- Take appropriate action.

I'll tell you the truth. The results I want to create don't include moving back into a home like the one The Nelsons lived in. I want to be one of the prosperous—happily sipping a Pellegrino on my balcony overlooking the ocean, visualizing my improved tennis serve. So what's my plan? Well, I *know* I don't want to be in the rat race of six billion businessmen competing to work for almost nothing, without nearly enough capital to go around, do you?

I will admit, for most of my adult life my focus has been on how to get myself into business, how to compete effectively, how to be the most effective marketer of my wares, and how to make sure I had access to enough capital to do that. Then technology made my universe smaller as my universe of competitors grew larger—from the 20 million people in the New York metro area, to the 300 million people in the United States. My focus moved from production and sales to finance and mass marketing.

Fortunately, I grew up on Wall Street, so investing in other people's businesses and allowing them to do the work came naturally to me. At age 40, inspired by my wife (the beautiful Elisea, the brains behind *The American Dream in a Box*), I built a great career investing in the businesses of other Americans, and teaching others to do the same.

No one is infallible, least of all me. But it has always been relatively easy for me to see where the money is and to understand the macro changes in the economy pretty early. Investing in other people's businesses, and teaching others to do the same made me financially comfortable, which means rich beyond anything a kid from the projects could have imagined. It's great fun, and I've gotten to spend my time with the smartest, most successful and influential people in America.

I've mentioned epiphanies, and I had one back around 2001. I could see that economic conditions had changed. Where the United States had once been a small, progressive, privileged marketplace, Internet and satellite communication was changing things—big time. Where a few computer wizards had held a near monopoly on new ideas and inventions, there was suddenly a whole world of competition. If you'd been one of these innovators in the 90s, you would have experienced what they did: Everyone needed your software or database in order to stay competitive, and your sales were growing at 100 percent a year! But almost overnight, there was a guy in Mexico who knew how to do it cheaper, a guy in Brussels who knew how to do it better, a guy in India who knew how to do it cheaper *and* better, and a hundred people in China who were bootlegging your software and selling it for almost nothing.

Now clearly, there are going to be great players and average players, but winning in business is getting to be akin to winning a medal in the Olympics. Clearly it can be done, but though many people try, not many succeed. And even the NBA's dream team—by far the best group of basketball players on the planet—was humiliated, when the guys took their dominance for granted a few years ago.

What I saw in 2001 has remained true to this day. Everyone who wants to kill himself or take boatloads of risk and is willing to tolerate any amount of sacrifice can qualify to enter the competition, but only a few will win. So who wants to do that?

I thought back to the stories of the gold rush in California. Thousands were crowding onto the goldfields, beating each other up, murdering each other to be first to stake a claim. Now, they all needed shovels, and once the fields became too crowded, selling the shovels became a better risk-adjusted deal than entering the competition. Chances were that the average competitor would have trouble finding enough gold to cover the cost of his equipment.

Cut back to the 21st century. The tool everyone needs today is capital. As industrious, courageous, and inventive as these billions of competitors around the world are, they were working in the fields for pennies five years ago, while we Americans have spent the past hundred years saving and accumulating surplus. Simply put, work is cheap, risk takers are a dime a dozen, but capital is unbelievably scarce!

For the first few years of this new century, Americans attempted to deal with this need for capital by creatively inventing new types of money. Securitization, credit default swaps, collateralized debt obligations—these are all newly engineered types of cash, designed to create enough capital to feed the hungry, developing global economy. And most certainly, this financial engineering will eventually prove to be the answer, right after more of us learn to navigate the complexities.

Some of us may not be able to throw a football 70 yards, but we do find this type of thinking easy to grasp—not many of us, but some. And there are going to be some false starts along the way, as we develop the global economy. Allowing the league of 150-IQ millionaire players to make their own rules, supervised by a very small number of underpaid 100-IQ regulators, is probably not a prescription for success, but I don't have a suggestion for the alternative.

Erase your old worldview: Competing in business is wonderful, if you have a product or service you love to deliver, and if you're inspired to compete for the love of the game. But as investors, here's all you and I have to be concerned with: The world needs capital. If we have some, the players, determined to compete, will pay huge premiums for it. They'll make enormous concessions and share the fruits of their labor with us, even putting us ahead of themselves in the distribution of profits.

In this generation, knowing how to get paid for the use of your money is going to be as important as risk-taking. Speculating on who is going to win the software, hardware, or biotech game will be about the same as betting your life savings on picking the next American Idol. Using your brains to get a better deal means knowing you don't always have to take that kind of risk to create the results you want. As Investor 2.0, you'll use your capital as a tool to allow others to:

(a) Work very hard.
(b) Take risks on your behalf.
(c) Give up a lion's share of their profits.
(d) Pay you before they pay themselves.

The playing fields where this is done are called the bond market, the money market, the shadow banking system, the bridge loan business, and other names yet to be invented. But the idea is going to be the same for a long, long time—maybe for the rest of my life. My job is going to be to help you get as comfortable as possible with this generation's good deals.

Investor 2.0 Shows His Skill

Compared to oil, natural gas is cheap. With an abundant supply and a slow economy, this is easy to understand. With the growth of the global economy continuing to pick up over the next couple of years, and along with that a demand for natural gas, investors sense a possible trade. Many of them will lose a lot of money because they'll be right about the economics, but they'll lose money because they don't get the timing of the trade right.

Once again you've been told that you can't time the market, but the truth is you'd better *learn* to time the market. Nothing else really matters, no matter how right you are. We only live somewhere between 70 and 90 years; being in the right place at the right time is all that matters to human beings. You don't live long enough to benefit from being right if your timing is bad.

As you see in Figure 6.1, there's a natural gas price spike every two and a half to three years. At this point in time (past mid-year of 2009), we're about one and a half years into it, so a lot of people are going to try the trade. They'll run out of patience as it moves slowly up, sells off, and generally moves sideways for another year or two. In the end, natural gas will spike, but most of the people who had the right idea will miss the trade. The price of gas will spike, because low prices are already leading to reduced production, gas wells deplete on their own, with production falling around 20 percent a year, demand will grow (or at least stay the same) and shortages will eventually develop.

Here's the irony of all this. If you were to just buy natural gas through an ETF and have some patience, and this spike is like all the rest over the last decade, you'd make 100 percent to 300 percent profit! Considering how much you usually make on your investments these days, that would be worth waiting a year and a half for, no? And if you did it through an options trade, you'd make 1000 percent! Yet, most people won't have a clue about what I just showed you. They frankly don't have the confidence and don't take the time to look at the facts from all sides.

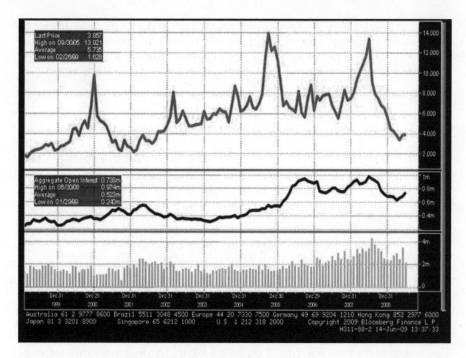

Figure 6.1   Pattern Recognition: Natural Gas Prices

The truth is I don't really know much about natural gas. I just happened on this relationship playing around looking at many different time frames and just looking at correlations. I happened to have some oil and gas expert on my radio program, he mentioned the relationship between oil and gas, got my interest, and I spent the evening fiddling around comparing them in many different ways, until I happened to run across this easy to understand relationship. Eureka! Finally an energy trade I can understand—and where I like the odds of being right.

I've learned from those rich folks that my money belongs in my pocket unless I have something compelling to do with it, with very high odds of getting back much more than I put in. This trade is worth my while. Investors 1.0 will simply hear on TV that the gas-oil spread is very wide. They'll go buy natural gas, or maybe even buy gas and sell oil. Then they'll get whipsawed around a little, become impatient, give up on the trade with a small gain (or more likely a small loss), and move on.

As Investor 2.0, you will have examined the whole relationship, and understanding the context, you'll not only have an investment plan, you'll also have a timing plan. If you get lucky, the trade will work faster than normal. If you don't, it'll take more time, but you'll just sit by patiently and enjoy yourself.

On the Air—*Quiet Please*

Side note to readers from announcer, Sal Monistere: If you remember, I took you aside during this book's prelude to give you a little insight into Dan's radio program. Shhh, come on in. Let's listen in on a conversation between Dan and long-time friend and colleague, Frank Cappiello. Dan is trying to draw a picture for the audience. The point? Insight into the thought processes of one of the first really famous investors: early Investor 2.0

(Commercial tag line—to full out. Music up. . . . and fade under for Dan.)

Dan: Well, happily that was a very short break. We're back with Frank Cappiello. Frank manages assets even now after all these years and of course has, I guess he basically invented the concept of being a television commentator on money. That was before CNBC or BizRadio or Fox or anything. And Frank, you were reminiscing about the first time when they had Wall Street Week with Louis Rukeyser as a prospective show in Maryland and how you came in and did the pilot for it and everything. What year was that?

Frank: It was in the fall of 1970 when we did our first program, and I was on every week as a panelist for about three or four years. And then they began to add more panelists and began to rotate, and finally I ended up where I was comfortable. Every three to four weeks I would do a show, and we did that for 32 years.

Dan: And you were the guy that stood in for Louis Rukeyser most of the time.

Frank: Yeah, sometimes. He was a hard guy to replicate, but I had my own style. I didn't pretend to be a broadcast personality. I think I'm a market guy. And I got more out of those programs seeing guys I knew on Wall Street every week or maybe every third or fourth week that would come on as guests and in meeting all of those guests I developed a lot of contacts. I don't think there was any single big investor that I hadn't met. With one exception, and that was Warren Buffett. Warren Buffett refused to come on Wall Street Week—(*Chuckles*) just didn't want to face Lou, I guess.

Dan: Interesting. Well, you know you've always done this thing and I admire you for it; there were a couple of you that were very good at that—uh, what's her name? Mary?

Frank: Farrell.

Dan: Yes, Mary Farrell was another. Just having that gift of being able to talk about this stuff. You know listening to you explain what's going on, you make it so obvious and easy to understand and it's so artful the way you do that; it sounds like you aren't doing anything. Yet there's so much to what you're saying. And then when you listen to other people do it—I'm telling you it's beautiful the way you do that and it's an art, and very, very few people have the knack for doing that. You know, I'm doing it now and I can tell you folks, it's not easy, very few people are able to tell such a complex story with such simplicity and economy as Frank. So anyway, let's talk about what you're buying. Now that you kind of think we're going to have a recovery—a slow one or whatever—what are *you* buying now?

Frank: OK. Well, we continue to buy into basically the financials, the banks, some health care, although it's very slow. There are not many good health care stocks around with all of the questions on what kind of health care we'll have. And we've been lucky by being very, very big on tech all during this period, really since January of '09. And I guess we've been focused on a couple of countries; I can give you some names if you'd like.

Dan: Yeah. But I'd like to ask you first: Even with that horrible economy and nobody buying things, no business investment, what made you catch on that there would be a technology rally and that technology would lead?

Frank: Well, early on, as far back as late last year, we felt that in order to survive companies were going to have to drastically cut their expenses. And also they were going to have to put money into things that would make them more efficient, that would make them more knowledgeable, etc., etc. Well, all of this is software computerization and so on, and the one we picked, as a matter of fact we've owned it for about a year and a half or two years now, is Apple. That seemed to us to be the perfect solution. Small companies would buy their computers . . .

Dan: And they were putting out a new edition of computers.

Frank: Sure. And the public, the consumer, if they were gonna buy anything they'd buy an iPhone, and Apple had a couple of other projects that were under way. And we felt that Apple was the strongest one to be in, and that turned out to be a pretty good choice. We also like Qualcomm, which as you know is a company that has a lot of 3G handset patents. And every handset practically in the world pays a fee to Qualcomm in one way or another to utilize the equipment. And finally our most recent purchase, it's controversial among the guys in the firm, we began to buy Microsoft in January.

Dan: You weren't necessarily a big fan of Microsoft?

Frank: No, I figured that Google and Apple both busted a lot of their future. But Microsoft was starting to do things that we find are very interesting. They're coming up against Google, and that's good for Microsoft. They need that competition, and they'll have some success with it. So we felt that Microsoft was a very cheap tech stock and that's the way it went.

Dan: OK, the other area you talked about was banks.

Frank: I think you have to have three or four banks in your portfolio really to make it over the next two years as performance develops in the banks. One is Bank of America, a lesser quality than the next one, J.P. Morgan, but Bank of America is very cheap. J.P. Morgan is not as cheap, but it's a better bank. And then you have to have Goldman Sachs, and I've had Goldman Sachs personally for two years and I've sweated over the stock. We have many of our clients in it; it was too risky until about the beginning of this year, and again that's where we said, "Well, of all of them that are going to come out running, it's going to be Goldman Sachs." They've already planned or announced that they were going to buy back, give the money back from the TARP. And that was an indication that, one, they could raise the money very quickly, and two, they had ideas on how to use it, and the results are history. I mean this last quarter was a blowout quarter. So that's the way our thinking has gone.

(*Theme music starts under...*)

Dan: Frank, I've gotta stop for another break. Can you stay with us through another segment? I want to ask you about how you actually get the fundamentals of these things. People have asked for it.

Frank: Okay. I'll be here.

(*Music continues under. . .*)

Dan: All right. Frank Cappiello will be with us on the other side. This is *The MoneyMan Report* on the BizRadio Network. Stay with us.

(*Music fades up to full. . . through segment ending, then out.*)
(*Go to break.*)

Note from producer Sal Monistere: How perfect, our editor said this would be a perfect spot for a chapter break, and look, we had to go to commercials anyway. Grab a sandwich, and then come on back and turn the page.

CHAPTER

7

Welcome to the Big Leagues

The Preparation: Homework is Critical, Roadwork is Crucial

I n this chapter . . .

- Cappeillo continues
- Go to Harvard, develop your contacts
- Read the papers and watch CNBC—Cappeillo, out.
- A weekend at Lake Wobegon
- Back to you, Dan and Dave

In The Studio with Frank Cappeillo—Part 2

Another note from Sal Monistere: So now that you've had a chance to go to the fridge, let's continue with Frank Cappeillo; he's talking with Dan about how to do the real work involved in analyzing a stock or a company. If you're seasoned, this may seem like Investing 101, but I'm betting that for most of you, Dan's guest has some very valuable tips. Shhhh. They're back:
(End of break—music under for Dan.)

Dan: My guest is Frank Cappiello, who has graciously agreed to stay on for another segment today. And Frank, by the way, you've been talking about what you're buying and selling, but if my listeners would like to read more of your commentary or know more about you, how can they find you?

Frank: All you have to do is link up with me by e-mail, and if you put your name in there, we put out a quarterly report on the market both past and present for the forthcoming quarter, and I'll be glad to send you some copies.

Dan: All right. Now, Frank, look, the other day I was talking about knowing how to win and I was reliving a conversation I had with champion boxer Jesse James Leija. Basically I'd asked him how on Earth a guy could tire out at the peak of his career—the way he did when he lost to Oscar De La Hoya. How could this happen? It's impossible. And he told me and my audience that it could only happen if you knew in your heart that you hadn't prepared properly—he called it the roadwork—then your mind starts to work on you; that's when it all goes down. If you've done everything you could, and you're at peace with yourself, you're never gonna get tired, you're just gonna keep on coming on. And so I was using that analogy for people who invest. Tell me, tell our audience—and I've had the question posed many times before—the question I had from somebody was, "Well, OK tell me how to do the work. Stop telling me the philosophy, how do I do the work?" So Frank how do you do the work? You're deciding that you want to buy Apple or something, you reason it out, but then you also find out about the company and you know a lot about it before you put money into it. Specifically, how do you go about it?

Frank: OK. Well, first of all, people have to remember that they're playing the toughest game in the world. I mean this is as tough or tougher than boxing or pro football. I mean it's very, very difficult because the stakes are so high and the competition is so stiff. But for those who want to try, begin with point one: the question is about the future. You know, what are the trends? What are the industries? Out of this fear of recession . . .

Dan: Hang on. How do you find that? You determine the trend for that industry; where do *you* go to get information like that?

Frank: Well, first of all you have to, you make a lot of decisions based on your contacts. Now a lot of the individuals who are hearing this just don't have the contacts we have. I mean, I went to Harvard Business School, and I developed relationships with a lot of guys who went on to Goldman Sachs and so on; they're still in the business, and they're *very* helpful. We trade stocks. We trade information. That's the first thing: to develop your contacts.

Now, developing your contacts at a cocktail party is not going to help. Obviously, most people can't just go out and develop these contacts. Fine, if that's the case, the first thing you do is you read a respected and very effective newspaper, one which I consider to be the best in the business is called *Investor's Business Daily*. It comes out every day, and gives you a complete overview of what happened yesterday, it talks about trends, especially trends in specific key industries. They have articles, and so on. If you read that continuously day after day for about three or four months, you'll begin to get a feel for the market and the rotation of the market, and some feel for what's going on on the inside of specific components of the market.

If you continue then to do it at least every other day, you'll have a continuous flow of information from some of the best people in the business, so that's number one. Number two: The *Wall Street Journal*. Same thing, you have to read it. And in the case of the *Journal*, you can just scan it very quickly for articles. And the third, and the only other newspaper I read, is the *New York Times*. I hate their politics, but it's the best newspaper in the world, and it gives you a lot of insights into the future.

Dan: What are you looking for?

Frank: The trend, the risks. What are the profits? And if you can answer those three questions, then you decide to buy the stock. The thing that people forget is, Warren Buffett has said this, others as well, there's one by Rothschild: "You buy when there's blood in the streets." Buffett says, "When your stomach is churning and you think the world's going to hell, that's the best time to buy," and he's exactly right. The best time to buy is when these stocks are down. The worst time to buy is on a day like we had today when the market is up 250 points and you say, "*Well, boy that stock is up 6 points, I'm gonna buy it tomorrow.*" No. Because all you know is what it did yesterday; you don't know what it's gonna do tomorrow, and in order to find out what it's gonna do tomorrow you have got to do some work. Ask your broker . . .

Dan: But remember your broker is based on a commission and it's in his interest to keep you moving around on stocks, which is not bad but you *know* he has a prejudiced point of view.

Frank: And for everything you see, you gotta ask yourself if it's *credible*. Are these people trustworthy? And you go on from there. There are a lot of rumors in our business and newspapers and the media; I mean you never see an article written about a man and a woman who've been together for 75 years, happily married—that's not of interest. What's interesting is this guy who's leaving his 50-year-old wife to marry a 22-year-old girl. I mean, the newspapers really frighten a lot of people, and I think they destroy a lot of faith because of this, because of their "head-lining" the articles that are inflammatory. But the papers I mentioned, the *Investor's Business Daily*, the *Wall Street Journal* . . . watch the nightly business report every night if you can and keep your eyes peeled on CNBC, even if it's only for 15 or 20 minutes.

(*Music up in background, under . . .*)

Dan: OK. All right, well, very good. And of course the best advice is go to Harvard Business School, make friends with the people who run Goldman Sachs, and just like J. Paul Getty "wake up early, work hard, and find oil." (*Both chuckle*) Frank Cappiello, thank you very much. And folks you can e-mail Frank and he'll gladly send you his materials. Frank, I can't thank you enough.

Frank: Thank you, Dan.

Dan: I'm out of time, I gotta go—news is next and I'll see you after that for hour number two. I'm Dan Frishberg, and this is *The MoneyMan Report.*

(*Music up full 'til break, then out. Cue news, traffic, weather.*)

Note from Sal Monistere: Don't go away; Dan'll be back later with more on this topic from his favorite stock-picker, Dave Dyer. But first, this word from our friends at Lake Wobegon.

The Lake Wobegon Fallacy

Lake Wobegon is a fictional town somewhere in the upper reaches of the United States, around Minnesota and North and South Dakota. It is the boyhood home of Garrison Keillor, the guy who, with tongue in cheek, reports the "News from Lake Wobegon" on a weekly radio show called *A Prairie Home Companion.* (It's been broadcast for years on public radio stations across the United States; they even did a movie about it.)

Now as the story goes, at least according to Keillor, in Lake Wobegon everything is friendly, everything is almost perfect—sort of like that fictional town called "Perfect" in those Walgreens TV commercials. Ahh, but in Lake Wobegon, all the children are "*above average*." Imagine such a thing!

This is about something I call the *Lake Wobegon Fallacy*, and the reason is because it's about people who think they're better than average. In their minds, they're better than average drivers. They're better cooks, better golfers, better chess players; they're better at just about everything. They're the majority of college guys who think they're handsome to a point well *above* average; in fact it's really about *most* people, because most people believe that they are smarter and generally above average when compared with most other people.

From this optimism that people feel about themselves, and their skills, and their ability to compete, from this comes something that totally shocks me. People with zero background who really haven't made a lot of money, who maybe ran a business and were lucky enough to sell it for something other than a loss, these people actually believe that they can take a single seminar on investing and then go out and beat the very best of the pros on Wall Street! And I'm talking about them beating the professionals who are doing things with the greatest of resources and the most experience in the world!

Yet here comes some plumber, who ironically believes it takes 20 years to learn how to solder a pipe (and he even went to welding school and had to go through an apprenticeship and everything), and this guy actually thinks he can go out there and become a trader or an investor and be successful based on a seminar, a book, or a $40 piece of software. Go figure. Trading and investing on Wall Street—and doing it successfully—creates millionaires and billionaires. It pays more than brain surgery; it's one of the highest-paying jobs in the world.

Look, I think people are perfectly clear about why it takes 20 years to learn to solder a piece of pipe. There are so many different conditions, so many different materials, and various thicknesses and temperatures and failure factors and just *tons* of stuff to affect the precise outcome. There are so many variables that as it turns out you just simply need a lot of experience to make good decisions about what to try, when to try it, what materials to use, and what methods to apply. Still, the successful investors and traders remain the best-paid people on the planet.

And typically our poor friend the plumber, like so many people, is bamboozled into thinking he can just go to a seminar and in a couple of hours or a week or a month learn how to outfox the smartest and richest people on the planet. How could he believe this? Because somebody sold him a bill of goods, a bit of snake oil. It was easy because we human beings are born with the Lake Wobegon Fallacy.

You know, every day you meet people who've created or helped build a business. Perhaps you've met someone who's financed a business that helps lots of people get what they want. These types typically have money, and some of them are very rich. Many of them financed these businesses through public markets and made lots of other people very rich. This is the function for which the stock market evolved. It works great!

But what a surprise that every day you meet people who entered the stock market for their own selfish purposes, who are just trying to scalp a little money by working the system, who really have no interest in helping anyone get what they want. Most of them have made zero progress over the past 10 years. Most of them are fodder for more knowledgeable, more experienced people. You know the old saying about the guy with money meeting the guy with experience?

Look, people who learn to trade (even novices) have a function in our economy, too. They add money to the system and help provide liquidity and fluid markets. I'm all for them. But most of these folks are now much poorer than they were a few years ago, which is why the BizRadio Network also runs one of the top trading schools in the country. I'm not anti-trader; I've been a trader all my life. I'm just against illusions (and *delusions)* of grandeur.

You know, the most expensive words in the English language are "Where has this been all my life?" This is what novices say when they try out a new idea and make money with it. They're convinced they've found the Holy Grail, and armed with confidence and good intentions, they ride into battle against the strongest players in the world.

We're all vulnerable to the Lake Wobegon Fallacy, of course, including yours truly. As I mentioned earlier, I was once thrilled to play golf with Chi Chi Rodriguez. I actually won a hole, and I'll admit that pictures of me on the seniors' tour ran through my mind.

Needless to say, I spent a lot of time working my way out of forests and sand traps. I wish I could say I just decided to go for it for fun. But the truth is I thought I was playing like the pros. I wasn't. The pros play within themselves. They select their strategy based on their strengths and weaknesses. They study the course, their own games, and their opponents' as well. Believe me, Chi Chi showed me that day that I'm far from being ready to play against the pros.

Based upon winning that one hole, betting him I'd win another would have been as stupid as a plumber thinking that just because he bought a stock and it went up, that he'd be able to do it again and again and compete with the guys who have been winning for a lifetime. I suggest you keep that Lake Wobegon Fallacy in mind every day. I do.

More from the Studio—Dave Dyer

And yet another note from producer Sal Monistere: OK, when we last left the studio, Dan was talking with Frank Cappeillo about doing the "roadwork" before diving into the arena with the pros, and we're talking about the stock market now. Great interview, but there's more to be said about the "nuts and bolts" of being properly prepared. Dan's favorite stock-picker, Dave Dyer had some thoughts to add. Let's listen:

Dan: Dave Dyer is here with me. Dave, the caller was saying, "I get the gist of what you say, but I need to know what you mean by 'the roadwork.' How do I start?" So Dave, tell us how *you* do the work. How do you know about these companies, where do you do your research? Spend a little time explaining.

Dave: Sure, you know, I really enjoyed that segment you did with Frank Cappiello because you got into some real practical specifics like the part about what he reads every day.

Dan: Right.

Dave: And that is exactly the sort of thing that, when I was first starting out as an investor, that is exactly the sort of thing that would have been extremely valuable to me. I wish I could have heard him back then. And I agree; the *Wall Street Journal* is fine. *Investor's Business Daily*, he praised it in great detail, and I really do love that one too; it's got all of the facts, all of the details. But what I wanted to say—in fact, while I was listening I almost called in. I wanted to say that if you just read what everybody else reads you are not likely to know anything.

Dan: You know that is exactly the subject that I was going to bring up with you today. I know some of the things you read, and I would like to have you go through a whole series of . . .

Dave: I have a couple of ideas here, a couple of things that I read where I find things.

Dan: But I want to go back to what you just brought up though, because it's a very good point. Folks, we are not saying that you should pore through there, look for news items, and then just because you heard about or read a good thing about some company, you run out and buy it. That is exactly what we are *not* saying.

Dave: Right. That was exactly the point I was going to make. That's what a lot of people do with the information and nothing could be more dangerous. It's wrong.

Dan: Exactly. Frank was talking about reading it all the time so that he can keep track of what's going on in certain industries, what the trends are in those industries, he said you can't just read the daily news to try to get ahead of the news. That's not gonna happen because by the time that story is in *The Wall Street Journal* and even *Investor's Business Daily*, it's done, that move has already happened.

Dave: It's too late, yeah. One of the things, there's a little magazine that I have read for years and—Are we broadcasting the video? I'm going to hold it up here so that people can see it on TV—it's called *Science News*. And *Science News* is run by a non-profit organization called The Center for Science and the Public, and it's been a non-profit since 1921. And basically it's a real good resource that gives you a summary of what's actually going on with fundamental research. It's written for the general public, so it's not going to be over your head. You know, they'll get off into high-energy physics and things like that, things that aren't likely to interest me, but in this week's issue, there's an article called "Tests Could Help Determine Who Has Appendicitis with Greater Accuracy." And this is a report, it was in a journal called the *Annals of Emergency Medicine* that I guarantee you I do *not* read. But now, I'm going to look at that and say, "*OK, here's a test that might help determine more accurately if people have appendicitis,*" and in particular it's useful for children because children may not be able to tell you, infants may not be able to tell you . . .

Dan: OK, that's exactly the kind of stuff I was talking about. See folks, now the next thing I want to do is, once you get that information and you've got that idea—well, I know what I do Dave, and I would love to hear what you do too. But the first thing I'm going to do is to go back over that thing, and I'm going to look at that company and I'm going to get their balance sheet. There are a number of different ways; you can go to Yahoo, it's a little bit antiquated, there is a much more up-to-date version of it available in places like Value Line, which you pay for, but you can get the same thing free at the library. There are a lot · of different ways to get that. You can buy reports from EDGAR and places like that. And of course they make quarterly reports to the SEC, but they're kept in EDGAR, those are called 10-Qs, and then they do the 10K at the end of the year. You can find out what the current information is—what I want to know is how much money do they owe versus how much are they making? It's not just fundamental research about the product; I also want to know about the company and its financial health and its ability to survive.

Dave:　You're out in front of me a little bit. And unfortunately, in this particular article it doesn't mention a company; it just mentions the name of the university that did this test.

Dan:　Sure, but if you really wanted to track that down . . .

Dave:　If I really want to track it down, I'd have to find out if that research was sponsored by a company, and then I'd have to find out if the company is a public company. That's the very first step. And probably 60, 70, 80 percent of the stuff that I run into like this, it turns out that the company is not even a public company, but it's all part of what you call the roadwork, Dan.

Dan:　I have got to stop for a break, Dave. This is a fascinating subject and we'll cover it more when we come back. We're also going to do your stock tip of the week, and we'll go over a couple of interesting stories on previous stock tips too.

Dave:　OK.

Dan:　OK, times up; we'll take a short break, and I'll see you on the other side with my good friend Dave Dyer. You're listening to *The MoneyMan Report* on The Biz Radio Network, we'll be right back.

Back to the Studio with Dan and Dave Dyer . . .

(*And we're back . . .*)

Dan:　Dave Dyer is here. We're doing his stock tip of the week, and we're right in the middle of a discussion about what things Dave does to get his fundamental information. Actually, I'm taking a survey of all of the people who are my most respected investors, people the audience could learn to emulate, and Dave's gonna do it a little bit more.

First let me check in at the NASDAQ market site. We're talking to Greg Hernandez from the NASDAQ market site right there in Times Square...

(*Greg and Dan continue through NASDAQ Report, then... Telco line transfer back to Dave Dyer.*)

Dan: OK let's get back to, well, let's see, there's somebody calling in, but Dave Dyer is on the other line. Dave, you were going to give me a little more info about what you think, uh, because Frank Cappiello said that in the end he liked the *New York Times.* You have another newspaper you like better.

Dave: Right. Yeah, you know, one of the things again, my theory is that if you just read whatever everybody else reads then you're probably not likely to have a big edge. So I try to read some foreign material, and in particular as far as newspapers go, I like the *Toronto Globe and Mail.* Canadian newspapers in general are very, very good, and you can read stories without the political overtones that you get from American press. So the *Toronto Globe and Mail,* which is available on the Internet for free, it's a great thing to read. The other thing that I watch sometimes is the Canadian news on TV. Now, we can't get Canadian TV here, and it's not part of any of the cable packages. There's some sort of a copyright issue, but you can watch the podcasts. And Canadian TV has a show called *The National* on CBC with a fellow named Peter Mansbridge, he's anchored that for ages. He's sort of like a Walter Cronkite. It's an hour-long news prog...

Dan: All right Dave, I guess we lost some time doing the market reports. I'm running a little behind, I've gotta stop for a break. And let's see, it's looking like we've overbooked this flight today, next hour's gonna be crammed, can you come back later on in the week and maybe we can talk about this some more?

Dave: Absolutely. This is really good material, and actually I was thinking I might wanna pick your brain on the same subject...

(*Music under . . .*)

Dan: Sure, OK. By the way, BNN is the one I was trying to think of, that's the station in Canada. That's the network that I'm on a lot and we'll talk about that. They're interesting in that they do longer stories just like you were talking about. The info is much more in-depth, and personally I think it's a good source for research also. Anyway, I'm up against the wall; you're listening to *The MoneyMan Report* on the Biz Radio Network.

(*Music up to full, hold, 'til time check, then out.*)

Radio Show PostScript

You know, coming off of that radio program with Dave Dyer, I'm reminded that we've dropped in a few stock picks here and there. I've got one more for you, and then a little later, we'll dive head first into a grand discussion on bonds. Just don't forget my initial disclaimer at the beginning of the book, page 1, Chapter 1. And if you've forgotten it already, let me repeat it here and often:

> *DO NOT go out and buy anything you hear about on the radio, see on TV, or read in any magazine or book, including this one, until you've done the roadwork, the homework, and the research necessary to be able to say the decisions were your very own. I'm not telling you what to buy, I'm teaching you how to think.*

That being said . . .

Alcon (ACL)

Everyone loves innovation. Remember when you first heard about the concept of laser eye surgery? It's amazing! They use a laser to create a thin flap in the cornea, the surgeon removes some corneal tissue underneath, and the flap is laid back in place. Presto! Instant eye correction. I once witnessed an actual surgery taking place and after 15 minutes, the patient sat up in the chair and said, "Wow, I can see that clock on the wall." Some points to ponder:

1. People in Third World countries are only just now becom-ing aware of contact lenses. The reaction is one of similar

amazement to that in the example above: "Contact lenses! Wow, no more glasses? Cool!"

2. Those middle-class societies are a growing number.
3. Proportionately they show a sizeable number of cases of vision problems and degeneration.
4. Alcon (ACL) is in the eye care business.

Alcon, Inc., develops, manufactures, and markets surgical, pharmaceutical, and consumer vision care products. They have one of the broadest product portfolios in the eye care industry, and they boast a leading market share in most product categories.

With operations in 75 countries, products sold in more than 180 countries, and sales of US $6.3 billion in 2008, Alcon is the largest, most profitable, and specialized eye care company worldwide.

Their focus, if you'll allow me the pun, is clear. They've been able to create value for their customers and the shareholders by constantly building on their position as the largest eye care company in the world. Alcon has worked long and hard to develop a reputation for introducing new levels of treatment and expertise to areas that lack basic eye care. It's a stable company, too, founded more than 60 years ago by two pharmacists in Fort Worth, Texas. Twenty-five percent of the company is now traded on the NYSE.

Alcon (ACL) is a big, solid company doing good work in a growing marketplace. This is a real international business. Based out of Switzerland, they're in a position where they can benefit from the expansion in the European economy, as well as the favorably low Swiss taxation policies. Money managers (just like you) are looking for attractive, big companies like this in which to invest. More importantly, as I stated above, the market they're in is a *growing market*. Blindness is preventable, cataracts are easily treated, and in many countries, they're *not* being treated. Alcon sells products for this business. There's a big demand for eye care services, it's still growing, and it will continue to grow in the Third World.

Nor is their marketing department blind (sorry) to the company's mission. This is directly from the Alcon brochure: "*We continually work toward a day when preventable blindness and other treatable eye conditions are no longer a threat to the global community.*"

Alcon has a giant market cap of $39 billion, and 15,000 employees all over the world. There are three divisions: (a) surgical, where they make equipment and supplies for cataract surgery and macular degeneration; (b) pharmaceutical, where they make antibiotic and allergy treatments for eyes; and (c) the consumer products division, where they are very well-known makers of contact lenses and supplies.

The focus (again, sorry) is strictly on eye care. Fundamentals are really spectacular, with a 45 percent return on equity and almost no debt. They have been a good steady dividend payer of about 2.8 percent, and they are not over priced (on a P/E basis). All of this, of course, deserves our omnipresent disclaimer, in addition to the one stated above. This one particularly regards timing: *If you're reading this beyond 2009, you absolutely are responsible for verifying all of this information, as you are responsible for always doing your own research.*

CHAPTER

8

More Skills, More Opportunities

Understand the Indicators and Develop
Appropriate Strategies

I n this chapter . . .

- Strategize, strategize, strategize—now say that three times.
- Big Chief Wrong Foot.
- How we even got to this point.
- Strategies I used in '09.
- Another epiphany—this time in the Green Room.

Strategize—Then Make Great Plays (or Play to Your Opponents' Weaknesses)

If you like to think of investing as a game, that's fine. I prefer to think of it as a serious sport. And I find that most of the players, like the insurance agents and the financial planners (those financial guys), are always talking about how you've gotta have a *plan*. But to them, a plan means knowing all of the names of all of the things in the game (the playing pieces), and having a lot of accounting stuff attached to the game.

What I'm talking to you about in this book, at my speeches, on my radio show, on TV, is all about making more money. Sure, you need a winning game plan, but there are a couple of different strategies. You've seen inferior football teams or basketball teams win by using a *competitive* strategy to catch the better players off guard. So, yes, sometimes you need a competitive strategy—*sometimes*.

But, that doesn't really work in, say, golf or target shooting. You have to know *which* game you're playing, right? Because this whole idea of just having a winning game plan isn't going to do anything for you if you rely on it in the wrong game or at the wrong time. If you're a golfer preparing to play a certain course, you have to have a course management strategy. It doesn't *always* work with a competitive game plan, because in golf and target shooting there *is* no competitor, you're playing against yourself.

On the other hand, a great attack or defense-type game plan works really well in tennis, boxing, football, and investing, because for you to win in those sports *somebody else has to lose*. On Wall Street you have to know how to practice *both* of these strategies. And you can win by making great plays yourself, or by playing to your opponent's weaknesses—that is, by helping the other guy lose. Both of those strategies will work.

Strategize—Win by Running Your Own Race

I'm always pleased when people recognize my abilities as an investor. There's nothing that makes me feel better than when they specifically ask me what my winning strategies are. It's not a short answer, but I can tell you this much: I don't go for it when the herd is stampeding in panic. I can short when I see it coming but not if it's already too far extended, that's when I have to be careful.

My point here is I'm not going to come out ahead by constantly feeling that I have to always be totally invested, but rather laying back and picking my spot to assume real risk. Remember, my goal here is to use my capital to help people get what they want, not to get caught running the wrong way. And I can tell you that you have to—again, my football analogy—double cover the great receiver; just know that if you do that, you're leaving somebody else open. If you put a lot of men on the line to stop the great runner, you may be leaving a receiver open. To me, Wall Street works the same way: You have to pick your spot, and you sometimes have to give up something to get something else.

Here's an example of giving up something. Let's say I see that I'm playing in a dangerous market. I see that the economy is about to roll over or that buying interest is starting to dry up. Now others don't see the same risk. Remember, just because the situation is dangerous doesn't mean something bad happens each time. You don't get killed every time you run across the freeway. Of course, eventually, if you keep doing dangerous things you *will* get hurt.

So I know that when I hold back because of potential danger, and the bad thing doesn't happen (and it often doesn't), the people who were all in will make more money than I do. More power to them, I say. They took a chance, and they won. People buy lottery tickets and get rich, but that's not a strategy that appeals to me personally, and I know living like that does not increase anyone's mathematical odds of success in the long run.

Now, every year, some sector or risky strategy gets hot, and those who took a chance on it, whether well-conceived or not, are winners. So every year, the people who took foolish risks and won have outperformed me. The thing is, a couple of years later, they're driving taxis because that kind of strategy does not lead to lasting success. Playing long shots catches up with you eventually. Remember the old NBA saying: "Live by the three-point shot, die by the three-point shot!"

Let me put this crucial point into the context of my life, not as an investor, but as just a guy: When I was in my teens, if I managed to get a date with some girl, I would absolutely run through a red light if I was late for the date because I just *had* to get there—compulsively I had to get there. There was so much of my self-esteem and my love of self wrapped up in whether I had the date with this girl or not. The truth was it was all about me and my self-esteem because I don't even remember who the girls were, and I know from experience that when I got there it wasn't all that good.

And folks, I don't run red lights now because I'm late for something. I realize that no matter how many times you get away with running a red light, you only have to be wrong once and the game is over. Again, the times I am willing to underperform the market are when the situation is dangerous, and yet that potential bad thing *doesn't* happen, and the stock market actually *goes up*. Those are the times I'm willing to give up outperforming in order to play my game.

Let's get back to my football analogy. The team decides what to give up in order to win the game. Are they going to give up coverage on the wide receiver? What about double coverage on the runner? These are strategic decisions that you have to think through. Most people don't do that. Again, since you're learning these tricks, these ideas, you can outplay the herd when the time is right; you don't have to run any red lights or be in a big rush.

That's the advantage that the great experienced investors—Investors 2.0—have: They know from experience that the opportunity will come, they know they can wait for their moment. Over time, I win by *not* making the big mistakes, and I don't give back the money I make when times are easy.

Understanding the Indicators

One of the great strategies you can use to find profits in the new global economy, and it works really well, is to *wrong-foot* the opponent. Sometimes you can actually wrong-foot the whole herd. The device I like to use is Leading Indicators. Now this is a very interesting strategy, an interesting state of affairs, because there's a ton of information out there about unemployment and manufacturing—all that stuff the government publishes—as well as figures about the economy. Companies publish figures about what they do, the industries publish figures, and there are manufacturing reports, think tanks, and on and on.

Take surveys, for example. There are figures everywhere, and yet when they get reported in the news they don't really help you make money at all. In fact, a lot of people say they can't figure out why they get a piece of news, but then can't really relate it to anything meaningful. They see it on television and think, "*Oh, boy, this means things are going down because unemployment is up,*" and then there's a big rally! The news doesn't seem to actually have any bearing on anything, and it doesn't help them figure out anything.

Well, here's why: Most people don't know how to *calibrate* all of these different statistics. They don't understand that the economic results that are being reported as though they are relevant are actually tied to the past, instead of indicating what is likely to happen in the future, like unemployment. And some of the other things they hear are actually indicators of what's *coming* in the future.

There are a few very good people who have studied the business cycle, one of them was Jeffrey Moore. His followers now run the Economic Cycle Research Institute under Anirvan Banerji, who happens to be a friend of mine. What these guys have done over a half-century or so is to calibrate the indicators. They've studied and catalogued and become aware of which indicators are lagging (they tell you about the past), which are coincident (they tell you about the present,) or leading (they help you forecast the future three months, six months, or a year out). But the news reporters who report the indicators don't really understand what they indicate. That is, they don't know how to help you sort out which statistics matter for your future investment strategy.

Think about unemployment. You often hear a report on employment, and it makes you think unemployment is getting worse, and that makes you think it would be bad for the stock market. And then when it isn't, you're asking why. But companies don't hire people because of some economic projections they see about nine months from now or six months from now. Companies hire people because the factory is already at capacity and they need people. Or they can't produce anymore and they have orders to fill—right now! And when they have to they go out there and hire people. So unemployment is really a lagging indicator, and it doesn't help you know how to invest for the future. It's that simple.

With this new employment activity, you know the economy will have improved, the company's profits will have improved, their orders will be up, and so on. But the stock market will have anticipated that a long time before you actually see any of the new hiring happening. That's an example of how calibrating helps you to avoid expensive strategic mistakes.

Think about this: If you have a depressed kid, what do you do? Give her a credit card and she goes to the mall and feels terrific, right? It all has to do with people having more money in their pocket; you know that, sooner or later, they're gonna spend it. And when they spend it they'll either do it by investing in something or by buying something, but either way they create economic activity. So when more money becomes available and gets into people's hands, that's a leading indicator. It gets much more detailed than that, but there's an example.

I've found that some of these think tanks, especially ECRI, are very, very accurate. Anirvan Banerji has been a regular on my radio program for many years, and he's given us tremendous insight because those guys have predicted every downturn and recession without missing one, and they've never had a false alarm as long as I've been studying them (at least the last half-century, but they probably go back further than that). They also study the entire world, not just the United States, and they can see waves of growth or waves of contraction moving around the world. Though big companies and governments pay big bucks for ECRI information, there's a lot of free information on their website. Using it gives you a real edge, once you get the rhythm.

As Frank Cappiello was telling you earlier, don't try to read a newspaper, get a tip, then invest. You'll always be late doing that. Instead, follow along steadily, get in rhythm, and soon you'll be one of the few who understands the trends as they unfold.

Now let's go back to the idea that these leading indicators help you wrong-foot the herd, or rather wrong-foot the market. The market isn't always right, you know. People say the market is right, but the fact is that if I know over the next few months that there's going to be a pick up in the economy, and I see a lot of pessimism and people are selling stocks, then whatever my purchasing technique is I have a pretty good idea that I'm going to be able to buy at a time when everybody is selling, and I'm gonna get a good deal.

Vice versa, we knew that the economy was about to start to contract, as we did in 2007, and we knew the economy was leading into a more difficult time, though the popular consensus saw strength. I remember so many debates on TV shows and panels, with others saying, "Show me the softness. I don't see any softness; look at the employment report, look at how strong everything is." And they were saying that at the close of 2007, when the economy went up by 6 percent. My God, what euphoria! And of course we later found out the country was really already into recession as that argument was going on.

Indicators—Wrong-Foot Part 2

When I first wrote this chapter in the summer of 2009, I was considering this whole idea of wrong-footing the herd and wrong-footing the market and catching people selling just as conditions were about to improve. I was basing my forecast on the study of that moment's leading indicators, which signaled clearly to me that the economy was going to show real improvement. I was engaged almost daily in debates that you may have caught on radio and TV. The consensus couldn't act on the improvement because it wasn't there yet, and most experts just don't know how to calibrate the indicators. At that time, they knew only that the decline had been slowing. "Less bad is the new good!" was the mantra of the moment.

Now I'm reviewing it in October, and the world already knows that the economy was about to turn mildly positive in the fourth quarter of 2009.

This whole idea brings up basic controversy because people will always say, "The market is right, just watch the price—the price is the key." Of course my comment is, "Sure the market's always right, because the herd is the herd." And if you want to know if something is going down or not, well obviously if it *looks* like it's going down, it's going down. If people are selling, it's going down. If people are buying, it's going up. The herd is the herd. They're obviously doing whatever it is that they're doing. But that isn't what gives you opportunity.

I'm about to tell you about the hardest thing for people to grasp. The markets do not care what is going on right now. They don't care about the economy, unemployment, the GDP, earnings or anything else. The markets care about all those things *three to six months in the future.*

On the day in August when I first wrote this chapter, I had just done a radio show with three of the smartest commentators on TV. You know them all; I don't have to identify them by name. But they were all unanimously pointing out how they didn't see any economic improvement as of early August 2009. I kept saying, "You aren't supposed to see it. It hasn't happened yet. The market is about the future!"

They all said, "Yes, we know that. We agree with it."

And yet, two minutes later, they'd be talking about the empty restaurant last night, and the sales going on in the stores. Even the smartest of us have trouble grasping this idea of calibrating indicators.

It isn't that difficult, and if you get it, you will have an unbelievably valuable edge at key turning points, when the big money is made.

Your opportunity lies in the communication between the members of the herd. How do the herd members actually keep track of what each of the others are doing? Why, of course, they use the media!

The process goes like this. The agencies of the government automatically compile raw numbers for you, right? And let's say for the moment that the raw numbers are correct. In reality, they're not, because they constantly get revised, but that's another issue. So, here comes a so-called expert. He's perceived to an expert and is widely believed because he's in the media. He doesn't really understand leading indicators and doesn't really know how to read the economy, but watch where your opportunity comes. When this expert, who has tremendous status and influence, this expert reporter, this media guy, reports *his* interpretation of the raw numbers, this is where the opportunity begins.

You see, the reporter is frequently wrong. In fact, one of the best opportunities, and one of the most harmful to most people, is when this media reporter gives us a second phrase or a second sentence that they use to explain the raw numbers. For instance, they'll say, "The stock market went down today 100 points... *on the bad employment data.*"

Here's the guy who is *the* tool for the transmission of data to the herd, the guy commissioned to disseminate it and have the herd understand it and be able to act together, and he almost always feels that the report needs that second sentence to explain it. Ah, but the opportunity for us lies in the fact that you and I know that the reporter is generally wrong—not about the data, but about his *reason*. We don't believe the reason he gives us because almost always that is *not* the reason that the move came.

Now, the next error (and the next opportunity) comes when the analysts and the strategists try to apply their own favorite lens or analysis technique, and their views are distorted by their own private biases and their expectations. When they apply those to the reported numbers that are being transmitted by the reporters and the government, it gets even worse. But for those of us looking for an opportunity, it just got better.

Strategy Lesson—How We Got to '09

Again, I can't help but address the financial and economic status of our world as I see it today. I'm sorry that you're not here as I'm writing; if you can't remember July 2009, go online and you'll see the condition of the markets and the world as I saw it when I looked out my window this morning. This chapter is about how we got here or, from your perspective, there. In any case, in order to see that I've gotta take you back a little farther to the spring of 2008.

Corporations were reporting strong results and tremendous visibility. Since then we've experienced a time that, for most investors, has been the most intense ride of their lives. As a group, as a united country, we've lost more money than any other time I can remember, any other time in my lifetime, really. So let's go over the situation leading up to July 2009. As I said, corporations look out as far as the eye can see, and in late 2007 they were forecasting very strong profits/earnings.

At that same time, we saw the leading economic indicators about to roll over. We saw things that happen six months before the economy and the market start to show strength or weakness. We saw how many loans were being made, how much money was being made available. We also added to the equation whether or not people were ordering things online or buying stuff at the stores. Those are the leading indicators, and we started to see some weakness there.

As far as the stock market goes, we could see that, under the surface, stock prices in many sectors were starting to weaken, even though for the most part the reported indices kept going up. Still, that period was looked upon by most as a bull market. And of course we continued to own stocks. But I was looking at the advancers versus the decliners (and here I'm describing the indicators) on something we call our "Market X-Ray." We were looking at the number of companies whose stock was going up versus the number of companies whose stock was going down—advancers versus decliners. And what does this tell you?

Well, when the number of advancing issues is rising, that means people are aggressive. People are feeling optimistic. They're actively looking around for more things to take risks on. They're optimistically looking for new ways to take risks and make money. When the declining issues start to rise compared to the advancing issues, that is, when the *number* of companies that are actually falling in price start to rise, that indicates that company by company, and then sector by sector, people are becoming more selective about their investments.

You also have to look at the amount of volume to the upside versus to the downside. This is an immediate cue that people are becoming more or less eager to assume risk, and it's often evident just under the surface. Remember that the indices are made up largely of big companies, which are often typical of the economy. But at major turning points we start to observe some underlying divergences. This shows up in the change in volume, upside versus downside. That was what we saw in late 2007 and early 2008, which flashed the early danger sign. Most investors couldn't see the danger sign, because index prices continued to rise for a while, but we started planning our exit.

Another great factor that tells you a lot about the underlying mood is the number of new highs versus new lows. When a company goes to a new high people are calling their broker and saying, "Get me in at any price, I'm so eager (so compulsive) to join this thing that I'm not waiting for any bargains. I want it now!"

Obviously a new low, especially on higher volume, that's when people are calling their brokers with "Oh, the pain is just *horrible*; you *have* to sell. I can't wait for a better opportunity to sell. Just get me out right now! I have to liquidate to the sleeping point." So these underlying moves tell us a lot about what's going on beneath the surface of the market, much better I think than the actual price changes that are happening on the surface. My friend Paul Desmond from Florida does a lot of research and gets the raw numbers for this kind of stuff, and he's really one of the best at this.

So we were discussing how we got to where we are today. Well, there was this other thing going on at the time. All of the company executives were being very optimistic. So were all of the analysts—you know, those people who don't really analyze anything, but simply listen to what the people in the companies say and parrot it back. They were all feeling very confident and strong. Never had they seen such visibility, never had they been able to look into the future and see continued growth that was so easy to read!

Yet the Economic Cycle Research Institute's leading indicators were on a path of sustained weakening. This is the institute that over the last half-century has successfully calibrated indicators in terms of whether they are leading or coincident or lagging, and they've learned to actually read the business cycles. As a matter of fact, they've done so with tremendous accuracy—forecasting every single recession with zero false alarms—it's an absolutely wonderful place to watch, read, and subscribe to.

So here we are with this terrific setup. Back in the spring of '08, while the experts and the people in the companies were talking about the maximum visibility and the most wonderful path ahead, the Economic Cycle Research Institute's leading indicators were steadily weakening. This is the *perfect* setup to get ahead of the market. The real leading indicators are weak while the herd feels great; now *this* is a profit opportunity building. So now as we move into the summer of '08 the Federal Reserve Board sees no problem at all.

In August, Ben Bernanke announces that he sees "a mild and short recession, if we have one at all." But by September and October we had a huge panic. All you heard about was "systemic risk" and "the entire financial system is ready to collapse." Take note: This was as we were coming into the election. And of course the real panic was the fear by the Republican government and the Congress and their appointees that the normal downturn would hurt them in the election. It was just coming out at the wrong time for them, probably due to earlier meddling. But regardless, here we are coming into the election in the late summer or early fall and suddenly it's September of '08 and there's a huge panic, particularly by the government (who was hoping to get itself elected).

And of course they meddled with the economy, doing everything they could to try to pour money into the banking system to stop the slide. But in meddling they made things a thousand times worse. Now, let me cut to the late winter of '08 and the beginning of '09. Here we are at the moment of maximum pessimism and panic. There were horrible reports by the chief financial officers of the companies. The Administration and the Fed were in a panic, calling for more power for themselves so that they would be able to remedy these things. This peaked somewhere around the first week of March 2009. Everybody was in a panic, and of course that's where the rally started.

It's easy to understand why because there just was nobody left to sell. Everyone who might take action based on this panic was already selling, and they were mostly right there at the bottom. For just a moment, forget about the events and stop being confused by what people say. Just step back and watch the mood of the markets as though it was a pendulum. You can see that at that moment in the first week of March it was clear that the pendulum was poised to swing back.

If you just disregard all the noise and all the confusion, you'll see that it's just simple physics. All you have to do is forget the words and watch the physics, and you'll be able to see the flow of energy. This is what I mean when I talk to you about focusing on what is, not what *should be,* happening. So now we come to the immediate past (and remember as I'm writing this, I'm living in a world as it is in July 2009).

The rally began on March 9, 2009, at the moment of maximum panic and pessimism (while, by the way, the leading indicators had already begun to turn upward). What we saw was an immediate big spike in demand for stocks. No, the economy wasn't improving, but stocks had gotten so cheap we were out of sellers. One good buyer was enough to move the stock prices up. You got lots of bargain buying, and that led everybody else to jump on the bandwagon. There were irresistible bargains, but even though it was a good rally, the selling really didn't go away.

The selling, which had stopped for just a moment, was resuming at each level. Sellers, who had wished for months that they'd been out of stocks, would sell at each rise in price. I went back to study all of the previous bottoms that preceded bull markets. I could see that not only does great demand develop because of the bargains, but that the selling stops and it *stays* stopped. Both sides respond accordingly: Buyers are active because they can't wait to assume new risk, and sellers hold out for higher prices. And they do this as cohesive groups.

But this time, after a very brief period, sellers were eager to unload, and after just a few weeks the sellers began to catch up with the buyers and the rally ended. Buyers were buying, yes, but sellers continued to sell.

Now, as we discussed previously, all throughout the herd everybody that had anything to do with disseminating information did his or her job to spread the *wrong* information. (It's the biggest weakness that the herd suffers.) As prices were moving up, the reporters gave us the right figures, always in a timely fashion, but they always had to add their own little adjectives onto everything. Why? Because they believe that makes better television.

They'd add their little adjectives onto everything, along with their totally inaccurate one-sense explanations. They'd never say prices went up today, rather they'd say, "Prices went up today on hopeful employment numbers." This is almost always wrong. That is *not* why the prices go up. And the reason they get it wrong so often is that once again they'd failed to calibrate the indicators; they don't know which ones are leading, which are lagging, and which are coincident.

They're too quick to associate whatever is going on today with whatever the market is doing, and they're usually wrong because they've just failed to calibrate the indicators. Then, after the reporters have done their job, the analysts take over. They take the misinterpreted figures and make up strategies based almost exclusively on their biases and wishful thinking. As we've said in other parts of the book, this is simply the way information gets to the herd.

The reason I have to keep alerting you to this and keep mentioning it is because, as members of the herd, we have a tendency to buy into that kind of communication. You have to really make an effort to be awake in order to avoid being fooled like this. I mean it's bad enough that our IQ goes down considerably when we become part of a herd. But because of the very inaccurate way of disseminating information throughout the herd, every member is being fed totally inaccurate or incomplete information! And now they each have a depleted mental capacity to actually act upon it! But I digress.

So here we were in the rally that began in March 2009. We quickly saw a 20 percent or 30 percent move, and that was immediately reported and analyzed as a new bull market. A new sense of euphoria spread over the herd. Ah, finally! Things are coming back to normal. But let me tell you something about this "30 percent move." It depends on your point of view. If a stock is at 100 and then goes down to 30, that's a 70 percent loss, or a 70-point loss. If you remain on the same scale, a 10-point move back is just a minor bounce. The pendulum makes this big arc, but if it only comes back a little bit, then it's a very anemic swing. Oh, but in all of the excitement and all the celebration, the media pass on this wonderful news that we have a 30 percent rally. It's definitely a new bull market, by definition, a new bull market! Congratulations!

You know, this is all just so simple, and it continues to be just as confusing as ever to most people. But it really continues to be easy for us, because, as usual, we're studying the herd, not studying the market.

Through all the back and forth machinations, experts have continued to speak with total confidence, as we have watched most of them get whipsawed horribly.

The great player doesn't make the guess if he doesn't have to. The great player waits. The lousy player feels obligated to make a guess. I mean, the average hitters try to guess what the pitcher is gonna throw next, but Mickey Mantle never tried to look into the pitcher's head and guess and neither did Ted Williams. These great hitters accepted the fact that they were receiving unconscious cues that their conscious mind could never be fast enough to handle. The spin of the ball, the subtle moves of the pitcher—the great hitter lets his unconscious mind make the judgment for him.

My Strategy at This Time?

For a long year, with a horrible economy already known to all players, with no indication when things might improve, with no idea how much of capitalism would be cancelled, with no idea how well the growing Asian economies would be able to hold up in the face of weakness in the west, the best strategy was to simply buy fear and sell happiness. That is, we assume that values will neither improve nor get much worse, and so every extreme move in either direction is wrong. If people get too happy, we sell them our stocks. If they get too panicked, we buy their stocks. Our time horizon is measured in days and weeks, and we never give back profits.

By late summer, our leading indicators had turned upward and were showing sustained, steady improvement for more than six months. At no time in history has a steady improvement in leading indicators failed to develop into real growth. Most of the world, and most of the experts most Americans rely on for their financial worldview, couldn't see any of this. In fact, by October 2009, most Wall Street experts were still mired in pessimism and depression, while the economy had already been showing steady improvement for months.

Looking ahead from October, I could only see more improvement in my economic forecasts, indicating that by the time you read this (spring/summer 2010, I hope) the economy will still be improving. Maybe by then, the experts will have caught up with reality.

This doesn't mean we are moving toward the kind of strong recovery we became accustomed to in the 1980s and 1990s, but I see the U.S. economy moving steadily toward real but modest growth.

Back when U.S stocks were priced for endless decline and depression, and with virtually all players skeptical about the recovery, I moved my time horizon out some. My guess (unlike me, you have the benefit of seeing what happened next, so you can make a judgment on how accurate was my thinking at the time) is that by late winter/spring of 2010, almost everyone will be embracing the recovery, the president will appear to be a visionary, and the markets will be anticipating continued economic growth forever!

I imagine I'll be selling stocks around that time, and moving my focus overseas, but we'll see. Hopefully I'll still be there on your TV or radio, giving you my forecast for the summer and fall of 2010, but if everything is great in the United States and everybody knows it, it will be time to focus on global growth.

Because I was patient earlier in the year, because I was able to rely on much less risky investments to earn income during the tough times, I patiently waited for the right moment.

In late 2009, I was willing to tolerate some fluctuation without taking immediate profits. I was ready for investing for meaningful appreciation, no longer just making short-term moves to take advantage of meaningless up and down vibration (volatility). In 2010, I expect to be focused on opportunities all over the world, and some disappointment here in the United States

When you read this, you'll already know whether the economy actually did improve going into the winter, but whether I'm right or not, you will be a witness to how one of the most successful nine-figure portfolios in the country is managed, and how the pros wait for their opening, More importantly, this book is here to equip you to apply that type of thinking to your own investment life.

And by the way, notice that this is how the real pros have always played it. Joe Montana played it this way, Elway, Federer, and the great Mohammed Ali. What they'd do is they'd set things up. They'd just patiently wait for that big opening, and when it comes they're ready because their concentration is there. It's the old Bruce Lee stance: ready, awake, alive. Not trying to read the mind of the opponent, completely relaxed, confident, ready, eyes open, senses turned on full; this is the stance of the black belt. This is the positioning of the pros. This is the mindset of Investor 2.0.

The Epiphany in the Green Room

Almost 20 years ago, I was waiting to go on a local television show (in fact it was the place where I was dubbed "The Money Man." I guess it sort of stuck). This was on the NBC affiliate in San Antonio, Texas, on something called *The Tanji Patton Show*. I was sitting in the Green Room waiting to go on and watching the show on the monitor. There was this story on about a bunch of psychologists who had done a study that the station's production staff thought was very interesting.

What they'd done that brought them to everyone's attention was a study on mastectomies, and it was in the news at that particular time because Nancy Reagan had had a mastectomy. Anything Nancy Reagan did at that time was news; she was a magazine-cover kind of a person. But this was a special story because by that time doctors were mostly doing lumpectomies, not mastectomies. In other words, they were removing the cancer, not the woman's whole breast.

The interesting thing they noticed was that once Nancy Reagan had her mastectomy, suddenly the number of mastectomies being given in the United States jumped an enormous amount. A whole wave of new mastectomies began to sweep the country. And of course everyone who had breast cancer (and read *People* magazine) decided to emulate Nancy Reagan and have mastectomies. But what's really interesting is that the doctors who had read the research and were supposed to know what they're doing were actually performing mastectomies in record numbers!

After about six months or so, this wild wave of mastectomies began to subside, and everything went back to the way it had been. The country went back to normal, and the doctors started to do lumpectomies again. And that's when this bunch of psychologists decided that this whole thing was worthy of a formal study.

Now, remember, the Internet was new and 24-hour television was new, so this was an opportunity to study the effect of irrelevant celebrity endorsements on the herd. It's what we've talked about here as a matter of fact: the transmission of faulty information to the herd. And that's why the herd loses money. But this was a bunch of psychologists, and what they found was very interesting.

What these psychologists learned was that when you get this kind of misinformation, it spreads like wildfire. It spreads very much like when you throw a rock into a pond and you can see the waves going outward. When you think about the eddies in a stream, it's almost impossible to measure which direction the individual molecules of water are going to go. It's such a complex movement and interaction between all of these different forces and molecules and gravity and all of this stuff.

But when you throw a rock into a pond, it creates a circular wave; you get "molecule group cohesion," and the water molecules kind of stick together and move together. They become very easy to measure, very easy to understand, and you can even start to see when the wave will subside. You can pretty much measure it and predict what it will do next. You can just see without applying any kind of sophisticated algorithms. Now, for me, this was a tremendous epiphany! I realized that my method of trying to understand and anticipate the movements in the markets was all wrong. I'd been trying to forecast what *should* be happening by watching the stocks and understanding their fundamentals just like everybody else. I suddenly understood that the thing to study was the herd of investors transmitting waves of information, very much like those waves in the pond. This was a study of *what is,* rather than *what should be* happening.

I noticed that if somebody said that a certain new invention was going to work very well (this was during the technology rally), and the word started to spread, there would be a rally and the stock would go up. And the fact is that the whole rally would happen and subside before anybody ever found out whether that invention was really going to work or not. It made it so incredibly clear to me that the way to understand the movements of the market was to study the changing moods of the herd. I'll give you another metaphor about this.

And look, I'm sorry for this big mix of metaphors. I'm trying not to mix them, but there are all of these different ways of looking at the thing, and I'm describing it to you the way it came to me that day in the Green Room on *The Tanji Patton Show.* I mean I leaned back and I started to think, "Gee, imagine there's this herd of cattle lazily grazing." Suddenly, somebody comes along and fires a gun into the air. Now the lead cow starts to run, and then a few of the others look up and see that one running and *they* start to run. Pretty soon all of them are running. Now, the herd leader doesn't even remember why he's running anymore, but he has to keep running to keep from being trampled by the accelerating herd behind him. So I'm sitting there thinking about how stock analysts and investment strategists (like me) are sitting and watching the herd running and analyzing the gunshot and saying, "Why, the cattle are wrong! There's no reason why they should be running. That gunshot wasn't dangerous at all." And these guys are studying the wrong thing! I realized I needed to stop studying the gunshot and start to watch the herd. I started picturing myself in a helicopter, flying overhead and watching the herd and trying to determine when it would change direction or even start to lose its cohesion.

As the stampede progresses, is the herd getting more and more out of control? Are they even more afraid now, and are others joining in? Because if they are, they're gonna run right through that fence! On the other hand, here I am in the chopper, and if I can see that they're coming up on that fence and some of them are starting to break off to stop and eat and they're all looking around and slowing down, then I can tell you that that fence is probably going to hold. And so the cattle, the helicopter, the fence—this was my epiphany. The fence represents what technicians call support and resistance points, and this is what really started this part of my career. It is wisdom, no doubt. And I'm glad to pass it on to you.

But I want you to understand something. There is a much greater principle here. The real reason I've told you this story is to hopefully make you see that people are prone to study the wrong factor. They put their money in and lose it to those of us who study the right factors. Frankly, they make it easy for us to take their money. They want to look at the market and the economy and they want to figure out what *should* be happening. And yes, maybe sometimes they're right. And sometimes they aren't.

But we want to study the herd, *not* the stimulus that's moving the herd. We want to read the market by studying the investors, *not* the market or the economy. We want to read what the people are actually doing. And the difference between what they're doing and what they should be doing is where we make the easy money. If you learn nothing else from this book, that's the one thing I want you to remember. It's what occurred to me that day at the TV station, what I call my epiphany in the Green Room.

Here's how I'll be applying this wisdom around the time you'll be reading this book. As I write the book, the world is just realizing that the stampede away from owning stocks has subsided, at least for a while.

I could see by measuring the buying power and selling pressure (the movements of the herd as seen from my chopper) that buyers have become more motivated, while sellers are getting more committed to holding out for higher prices. This is leading me to buy stocks, while others still don't see the improvement in the economy.

My forecast is for a modest economic recovery, but with foolish business, tax, and economic policies being implemented by the U.S. and many European governments, I don't see how the recovery could be as robust as the ones we became accustomed to in the 1980s and 1990s. So as the skepticism turns to belief through the coming winter of 2009, I'll start to grow more cautious. In late summer of 2009, only around one out of six investors believed in any kind of economic recovery for the United States. In October it was more like one in four. I suspect that by next winter almost everyone will believe in the recovery. In fact, because of the tendency to extrapolate, I expect to see excessive, inappropriate enthusiasm.

When I start to see the prices rising, but the underlying Market X-Ray weakening, I'll fight my own herd-generated enthusiasm and begin to sell stocks. I'll be looking for the number of advancing issues on the New York Stock Exchange to start to lag behind the prices, as the number of declining issues starts to shrink. This will tell me investors are becoming more selective, and this will gradually morph into outright selling or distribution.

I'll also be watching for the upside volume to start to shrink as compared to the downside volume, telling me that while the main stocks in the indices are still doing OK the desire to assume risk is on the wane. When I see these underlying signals, I'll start to put tight stops on my holdings, and let the market itself take me out.

Here's another underlying signal I'll be watching for. As I write this chapter, I notice that whenever stock prices in the United States rise, the dollar declines in value and vice versa. This relationship has been consistent for months. Now I expect our economic recovery to turn out less robust than people next winter will expect. But I also expect China, India, and much of the developing world to be strengthening. Many of those countries are putting policies into place to attract capital, just as we in the United States are doing our best to chase capital away.

So as those countries' development picks up, their demand for building blocks such as copper, steel, iron, coal, fertilizer, and the like should increase, pushing up those prices.

If the U.S. stock market starts to weaken beneath the surface in the way I've just explained, but the dollar goes down in value instead of rising, and the prices of those raw materials starts to rise, I'll shift my holdings from U.S. stocks to mainly Asia and raw materials.

I'm not sure what will happen in the future. I'm not a fortune teller, but this chapter should give you a good deal of insight into what kinds of things you should be watching for as you grow into Investor 2.0. Now, get out there and do some roadwork.

9

More Strategies

Deciding How to Get out Before You Get In

In this chapter...

- Stopping your losses
- Write down the conditions
- Ulysses: "Untie me? Don't you dare!"
- Let's hear it from the experts
- Keeping your profits

Rules of Thumb—To Be or Not to Be?

Stop-losses. You have to set them. A rule of thumb? This is a big issue, because teachers, advisers, and all manner of experts have learned this rule from each other, and pass it on to the rest of the herd as though it were one of the Ten Commandments.

You must know that the more human beings hear an idea, the more they accept it as fact, and the less discriminating they are about believing it. The chorus of experts will all tell you that in every trade you do, you must, without fail, absolutely, positively, always set stop-losses. This means you should have an automatic rule that when you make an investment and it goes against you by some arbitrary number (8 percent seems to be a popular number for this), you must sell out.

I'm going to surprise you. I'm going to tell you that like every attempt to oversimplify life, sooner or later, trying to live by rules of thumb will end up costing you money. Investor 2.0 knows there is much more to this discipline than simple rules of thumb.

Look, I agree that discipline is critical. You'll never be sure you're doing the right thing, and you generally don't want to let a small mistake turn into a large loss.

I've compared notes with the best traders and investors on the planet—people who are on the front lines doing this stuff daily and dealing with billions of dollars. We've all agreed that no matter what our plan is, no matter how intelligently we conceive that plan, when the time comes to execute, you'll almost never feel like doing it. You don't *ever* want to buy when everybody is selling (or vice versa), and the reason is because you have the same instincts and as a result have the same impulses as the rest of the herd.

Why? Let's say I've had my eye on a stock for months. The market's been good, I'm feeling good, and I'm in that expansive mood where I'm having great ideas. Also the best stock-pickers in the world are bringing their buy ideas to my radio show every day, and this is one of Tobin Smith's favorites. I mentioned ChinaTel earlier, and now I'm ready to take action.

I've taken that idea from one of the best stock-pickers on the planet, and put my team on it. We now know as much about that company as anyone alive. I know what the chosen company does, I'm positive they have a great future helping people get what they want, and I'm sure sooner or later they'll be a winner. But you see, that's how I feel when I'm at peace, expansive, optimistic, and thinking about my future strategy, waiting patiently for the stock price to come down to a low-risk entry point.

Now cut to a couple of months later. Stock prices in general are now falling. Things are going down, prices are lower, and my target stock is approaching the point where I planned to buy it. But the markets don't just go down. They go down accompanied by bad news. The media—the tool for the transmission of information around the herd—is full of bad news.

You must remember what prices are for our herd. Prices are the shortcut signal for telling what the situation is. Prices falling in a free market are there to indicate problems. When the value of things is falling, people are generally saying bad things about them, and that takes them down farther. The bad news is like a fungus. It grows upon itself, and boy oh boy, you *really* hear about it.

"Unemployment is up, and the gross domestic product is down. Nothing is good," and on and on. The media reflect back what they think you expect. So here I am, I'm getting my signal that says it's time to buy my target stock. It's come down just as I expected, and yet I just don't *want* to. I'm not ready. I don't *feel* it. I'm experiencing the telepathy of the herd. And that same thing that goes for a buying situation, goes for selling.

Let's say I've been smart enough to write down my plan, so I buy the stock at the price I was waiting for, during the inevitable moment of general distress.

Now why would you or I ever expect that our plan would pick the exact right moment in the cycle—the exact bottom tick—to buy the stock. We know we've identified a terrific company, with a leg up on the competition. We've waited for a moment of distress to snap it up at a discount price. And lo and behold, the market continues its decline for a couple of more weeks. I bought that stock because I expect to provide capital to help millions or billions of people in one of the fastest growing spots on Earth to get what they want. Do I really think I have a crystal ball that will identify the exact bottom or the exact right moment in time to provide capital to that great mission?

If I adopt a plan that depends on that level of precision to win, I'm just setting myself up for frequent losses. My mom used to warn me when I was a kid trading silver contracts to make it through college, "I know you think you're a genius, but any plan that requires you to outsmart the rest of the world in order to work is a LOUSY plan."

If I set myself up in a plan requiring unnecessary precision, how many times will I have the right idea, buy a stock that eventually makes a fortune for its investors, but lose money because I missed the timing by a week or two?

Now, here's where most investors get hopelessly confused. If you're going to systematically sell out when the market comes down by a set percentage—the great William O'Neil suggests 8 percent—how can you ever buy down? And how can you patiently wait for your well-thought-out, wisdom-filled plan to work?

Look, if you're investing your money with courage and commitment, helping people around the world get what they want, and you love the company at $20 per share, don't you love it more at $17? I know I do! So how can you reconcile the strategy of applying tight stop-losses with a commitment to live your life with courage and conviction?

This is a source of confusion that has turned many smart, otherwise skillful potential warriors into cab drivers. For half a century, I've sat through the endless debate between wonderful traders like

John Murphy and wonderfully successful investors like Dr. John Rutledge and Frank Cappiello. Well, I'm going to reconcile it all for you right now.

A successful warrior doesn't win because he isn't human. He wins for precisely the opposite reason. He knows himself. We don't act on our feelings and impulses at the moment of battle. We don't want adrenaline to determine our next move.

In advance, let's write down the conditions that will trigger the strategic buy or sell. That way, we'll force ourselves to do it. This problem has been separating the great warriors from the mediocre as long as humans have been relying on combat and competition to better their lot and build their territory.

Remember Ulysses ordering his sailors to lash him to the masthead as he sails past the Sirens. "No matter what I say, no matter what I do, by no means release me until we have passed the Sirens' Island."

So, let's get back to our example. I've planned in advance to buy a stock representing ownership in a company that I believe helps people around the world get what they want. I've been patient because I learned about the company at a moment of societal optimism and confidence. I knew the mood of the herd would eventually turn. I knew the stock was much riskier at that high price level, and I thought there was a good chance I could get it cheaper after the herd's mood inevitably turned more negative.

I also knew this wasn't a frivolous trade. I have conviction, and I understand exactly why I'm willing to take the risk. I think there's a huge profit in store for me and the target company. (Apple is a perfect example in the technology field. Blackrock, Goldman Sachs, and the Blackstone Group are perfect examples of financial companies about whom I have the same great conviction.)

I don't want to be right and lose, and in this case the large profits I anticipate are worth my patience. As an experienced investor, I don't want to get snookered into allowing my success to be dependent on perfect timing. I know there are other great players lurking around every corner waiting to take my money. I know why I'm making the investment, and I want to be as certain as possible that my play is as good as my strategy. So I make the decision.

I'll split the money I am allocating to this trade in thirds. I choose which risk I'm going to take. In this case I choose to take the risk that I don't put as much money as I planned into this stock. At the moment of truth, when the herd has taken its inevitable swing from euphoria to distress (taking me along with it), I'm ready to make my move. I don't feel like doing it, but because I'm a seasoned pro with a written game plan, I *will* do it.

I'll commit one-third of the allocated money to buy that stock when I think we've reached maximum fear and negativity. Since my mind is open and my senses are alert, I have a feeling for how the herd is feeling, because I'm one of them. I'm pretty sure I'm right about the company and its future, but I'm less sure I can catch the moment of maximum fear. So I've prepared for the possible error by keeping most of my money in reserve.

Now if the stock takes another significant dive I can throw in more of my money. I can buy down. I'm totally focused on this game, so there's room for another drop and another buy. And if the mood starts to turn more positive, I can catch that change early and throw in the remaining third of my money. Remember, I made the choice to be willing to win smaller if the stock started to run up right after my first partial buy.

But understand, there are other reasons for buying or selling a stock, a commodity, or anything else. There are formations or patterns that brilliant traders can learn to identify. They see a certain kind of dip, a certain kind of gap, a certain kind of motion that they've learned to navigate. They have a feel for this gambit or combination just as a great chess player can identify a certain pattern or combination and use it to take his opponent's queen. He can feel what the competition is about to do because he's seen that setup before. We teach people to identify those kinds of opportunities, and as new traders become more experienced, they learn trades they can repeat over and over, and pretty reliably make money on them.

I worked my way through college and out of financial trouble many, many times in the early part of my life using such techniques. They are real.

However, if you think you've identified a pattern, made your move, and it turns out the other team doesn't do what you expect, you'd better be wise and disciplined enough to admit you were wrong and abort. In this case, you're playing against the other investors or traders. The stock or commodity is just a chip. You have no commitment to a mission to help people get what they want. Some kind of system of stops is the only way to have a long and prosperous life when you're using those kinds of strategies.

I see no conflict at all and no inconsistency. These are two different types of situations and two different standard operating procedures.

Studio Time! "And now, back to you Dan . . ."

Another note from Sal Monistere: Time to take a peek back into the studio for another segment of The MoneyMan Report. *It's Tuesday, that means "Genius Meets Street-Smarts" is up and that means TWO special guests; Dan welcomes Dr. Arthur Laffer as well as Dr. John Rutledge. Get ready for* The MoneyMan Report *on the Biz Radio Network!*

(*Music up, then fade under—Cue Dan.*)

Dan: Thanks, Sal. OK, let's get started. Dr. Art Laffer and Dr. John Rutledge, I promised our listeners a lot of wisdom today, because both of you guys advise billions of dollars with a "B," and perhaps trillions with a "T." I'd say between the three of us, we've made just about every mistake you could make; I'm sure I've made the lion's share of them myself. Now we're here to help you avoid these same mistakes. So the subject matter I want to discuss with you two is about putting stops on. It's something that's taught regularly by the guys who teach trading and technical stuff, in the event that an investment goes in the wrong direction.

Now take *Investor's Business Daily.* William O'Neil is a brilliant and influential investor/trader and probably a good friend of each of you. His books teach people to put a stop on after a stock goes down by 8 percent, which for me is a very stiff and structured way to do things. When you guys make an investment and you see it going the wrong way, what do you do about it? Do you use stops, and if so how do you structure it, and if not, what do you do instead? And that question is for both of you.

Arthur: Well you know Dan, they say the definition of experience is recognizing a mistake when you make it again. (*Chuckles*) So I'm not really the right guy to give you all this advice on how *not* to make mistakes, 'cause I'm still making as many as I always have, but what I don't like is living by some arbitrary rule. I don't think that really makes sense. You have to think about selling the asset before you buy it. What circumstances might happen, and what would you do in those circumstances? If you fail to plan, you really plan to fail, and I'd advise considering how you'd get out of an asset before you even think about buying it. John, does that make sense to you?

John: Sure it does. You know, my investment skills really were developed in the private equity business where it's very difficult to get out of things, period, and you frequently own that stuff for three or four or five years. Look, it's only when you burn your own fingers that you become sensitive to the heat. Just like Arthur, when one of my teams comes to me and says, "We really should buy this company," I'd always ask them, "What's the bet you're making? What do you think is going to happen that's going to make this thing better than all the other investments out there?" Then I'd ask them what could go wrong. Sometimes you're betting on a certain policy change to take place or a certain technology change, but the market doesn't allow you to make big amounts of money every day, so you have to have some special reason why you think it's gonna do well. It's not very forgiving when you make mistakes.

Dan: Right John, can you tell our audience specifically how you do these stop losses?

John: Sure, I sit on these prices every day, and when they're moving the wrong way before I pull the trigger, I always ask myself what was the fundamental bet that I made, and do I still believe it or has something changed to make that bet wrong. You can also change the size of your bet—that way when you're wrong (and you will be wrong), you won't lose too much of the portfolio on any one of them at one time.

Dan: OK, John, I'll tell you what, let's talk about an investment that each of you has right now, that could potentially go wrong—something liquid, where you've either bought it or sold it and can reverse that trade. Now I categorize it that way because John you're talking about private equity, and of course many of us like it better. You only have to worry about whether you're gonna make money on it or not, you don't have to worry about the psychology of people and how they're going to feel about it two or three years from now. I know that's a harder game for *me* anyway, but both of you are making investments now in public markets of things that are liquid, so let's discuss any provisions that would be the equivalent of a stop-loss. John Rutledge?

John: Well, I'd like to talk about a China bet, because in April I was in meetings in Haikou, which is a little island that hangs down between Hong Kong and Vietnam, meeting with some of the Chinese leaders. And I learned things down there that convinced me that China was returning to growth faster than people were saying. I have a bet on the growth of China.

However, when you bet on China, you have to remember that they're not so good with property rights, rule of law, courts, judges, and all those other niceties that we have in our market, so you have to be cautious.

(*Music sneaking up in background.*)

John: I have a bet on the Shanghai Stock Market, that's an Exchange Traded Fund (ticker is FXI), which are stocks that are *in* their market and therefore subject to all those risks. So that's quite a small bet.

Dan: OK John I need to ask you to hold your thought right there. I have to stop for a break here, but we're gonna come right back. I want you to finish that story. And Dr. Laffer, this break will give you a chance to gather your thoughts; I know you've got a story to tell also. We're sharing the wisdom of two absolute giants in the financial field, Dr. John Rutledge and Dr. Arthur Laffer. I'm Dan Frishberg. *The MoneyMan Report* continues in a minute, don't go away.

(*Music up full to end.*)

In the Studio with Dan, John, and Art—Part Two

It's Sal again; let's get back to The MoneyMan Report, *with our host, I mean author, Dan Frishberg:*

Dan: We're back with Dr. Art Laffer and Dr. John Rutledge, as *The MoneyMan Report* rolls along. On my VIP line, Dr. John Rutledge, we were lucky to catch him just before he boards a plane to go over and advise the vice-premier of China, also Art Laffer, the man who essentially brought supply-side economics to the world. They're both here with us, providing a little wisdom gleaned from nearly a century of combined experience of investing. Art, it was your turn, talking about some investment you're in now and what's the basis for your decision about what to buy, why you're buying it, and what signs do you look for to tell you that you might have been wrong? And more importantly, what would make you reverse it?

Arthur: Yeah, Dan, well John made the point before. I really do think that there's more coming inflation and a weak dollar. The way I've sort of protected myself from that inflation, what I use as a hedge is, I bought the TBT Daniel. It's an ETF that's a double-short on the government long bond, so if interest rates go up I win, if they go down, I lose. I bought it with U.S. Treasury rates at about 3 percent and made some money on it, now the yield's come down again. It's down today, and my decision is whether or not I should sell it. Do I have a stop-loss on it where you say, "Get the heck out"? And you know, I don't like those rules either, you know like somebody said it was what, 8 percent?

Dan: Yes, that was William O'Neil.

Arthur: Right, William O'Neil. Well, I have great respect for Mr. O'Neil, but I don't agree with that. Like John, I asked myself if I still think this is a correct bet and whether I think interest rates will go up. In this particular case, I *do* believe interest rates are going up, I *do* believe inflation's a real threat, and therefore I *don't* want this out of my portfolio. I really don't have to know to the moment or to the dollar when or how much rates will rise. I just believe strongly that they will. A little move one way or the other, in the absence of major changes in policy, means very little to me. My decision right now, Dan, is not whether I should sell it, but whether I should double-down and buy some *more* of it. Now I've just got it as a hedge right now, but I'm thinking of buying *more* of it, making it an investment, and selling some of the assets I'm using it to protect.

Dan: Wait a minute, that's very intriguing. I'd like for you to explain that one again.

Arthur: Right, well I've got some stocks and other things that will go *down* if interest rates go up. So I bought the TBT really as a hedge against those stocks.

Dan: You bought the negative treasury, it goes double the opposite of Treasuries.

Arthur: Yes, so if interest rates and inflation rise, I've sort of hedged my portfolio of stocks. What I'm thinking about doing right now is selling off some of those stocks that have done very well, taking those proceeds, and putting more into the TBT. It has fallen back some more, and I think it's a good buy once again. Does that make sense to you?

Dan: It does make sense, but I guess my question would be then that you see a correlation whereby you would find it difficult to imagine a situation where stocks go down without interest rates rising. Or vice-versa, is that correct?

Arthur: That's correct Daniel. I believe that higher interest rates really do hurt the stock market, and what I'm doing is hedging. But now, I'm thinking that betting on those higher interest rates is really a good investment rather than just a hedge.

Dan: That's interesting. Let me see what John, John, any thoughts on that?

John: Yeah, Dan let me chime in on that. You know, in the private equity world, when you buy companies, you buy them by trying to value their ability to produce future cash flow, which is the goodies you get by owning a company. The way you translate the future cash flow to the valuation is by using an interest rate, as Art's describing it, to discount it. And when you look at the S&P 500, as an example, and say, "How long do I have to wait to get those cash flows?" that number is called the duration. And the duration of the S&P 500—more or less, the weighted average of its future cash flow timing—is 26 years into the future. Which means today, if the long-term treasury bond interest rate increased by 100 basis points (one percent), the value of the S&P 500 would decrease by 26 percent, so that's a huge price to pay! So back around to your original question: I think what both of us are getting at is that the way you should invest is by first figuring out the thing that is what you personally know how to do well and have the time to do. You know, in our case these are issues where we spend a lot of time, and we don't want to delegate that decision away to a rule—even though someone else might find that worthwhile to do.

Dan: Well, I'll tell you I'm listening to this and thinking, "Well, gee, I'm not an economist. I'm an investment strategist, but I could imagine a situation where the economy was doing very poorly, the stock market went down but there was no loan demand so interest rates stayed down." Do you see that this could happen too?

Arthur: Sure, Dan, absolutely. (*Chuckles*) All sorts of things could happen.

Dan: Well, I couldn't agree more. I hear music, that means our time is up. It certainly doesn't mean I don't want to go on with you two. I do hope you'll both be back.

Arthur: Thank you so much, Daniel. John, enjoy your trip to China!

John: Thank you both very much. I'd love to come back.

Dan: Then that'll wrap it up. You're tuned in to *The MoneyMan Report*, I'm Dan Frishberg, and I'll see you tomorrow.

(*Theme music up and out—Cue news, traffic, weather.*)

A Notation of Ultra-Importance

The hall-of-fame players above have been sharing with you how the real guys really manage adversity, as opposed to the simple "rule of thumb" behavior of the amateur or pretender. Here I want to rehearse what you will inevitably go through, and let's practice how to handle the special situation with wisdom, courage, and discipline.

If the mood of the market or events turn out to be worse than you expect, and you've thrown in the whole allocation, and the stock keeps declining, DO NOT EVER INCREASE YOUR ALLOCATION IN THE MIDDLE OF THE BATTLE. This is a much more sophisticated and precise type of stop-loss, suitable for a warrior who plans to come home from battle as a richer man. When you're playing on the big stage for millions of dollars, you know you'll come home either rich or dead. (I pick rich.)

The other stop-loss that must be applied to this game is to write down the conditions that made you buy in to begin with. Be as precise as possible, because the moment you see those change you must sell out, win or lose. Before I make a move, I'm going to think through all the possibilities, and put down the odds of different outcomes and different fluctuations along the way. In a volatile, moody world, given to a lot of vibration, the chances of a meaningless 10 percent price move in either direction or both directions is very high. In a typical trade/investment/transaction, the simple quantitative rule-of-thumb stop-loss would have given me a 67 percent chance of losing my money and being "stopped out," even though I was totally right.

When you know why you're making the trade or investment, and it's about a conviction that you are using your capital to help millions of people get what they want, you'll be out of the game very early if you allow yourself to lose your money through some amateurish, fear-based rule of thumb, black box system. But, that isn't the only type of trade or investment that can work. You have to master every tool to win in this high-stakes competition against six billion others.

Let's return for a moment to talk about the technical trade, which has just as much validity, but is totally different. Personally I engage in both types of trades/investments. I don't even bother to have a preference anymore, because for me it's not about what I like, it's about what the situation or the opponents give me.

Sometimes you just notice a pattern. I've mentioned the great trader Vince Rowe, who has noted that on a daily or hourly basis, the price of Starbucks stock is correlated to the price of the commodity coffee. This is not trivial, it's brilliant. He will not make 100 percent on his money in one year-long trade, he can make the same 100 percent on 20 low-risk half-hour-long trades throughout the year. If the previous move—helping millions get what they want for big profits—is hitting the driver off the tee, then this coffee/Starbucks trade is the pitching wedge. And by the way, the great gladiators in the game of golf will tell you, the short game is where you make the dough.

In the case of a simple pattern-recognition trade, you must observe tight stop-losses. If you committed your money based on a pattern, and the pattern doesn't work immediately, you get out—period. You never adopt a new story in the middle of the game. You strap yourself to the mast, like Ulysses, force yourself to ignore the Siren's song, live to win your battles, and come home rich and famous. These are the warriors we tell our children about.

Rule 1 (Never Give Back Your Profits in a Tough Market)

One more important place I've learned to always use classic price-type stop-losses is in a very tough stock market, such as the one we've been living through in 2008-09. This is not the time to be greedy. Consider yourself fortunate if you get something right and score in a tough market like this. Ignore what you wish. Ignore the fact that you hope to win big, long-term profits. If you buy a stock and the price goes up, and then you see the mood of the market rolling over, set very close stops right under the current price. Ride the price up a little further if things go that way, but let the market take you out of the trade, if it must. Do not, in a tough or doubtful market, give back profits. This is where judgment comes in. I'm going to be flexible enough to let my plan work, but be very rigid about giving back money I've already made. Again, this is a rule for a tough market, not a constant.

Many less-experienced amateurs will be so eager to preserve the win that they sell while the stock is still on the rise, because they set some kind of predetermined sell level: "If it goes up 15 percent, I'm out." For as long as you and I are together, I'm going to keep reminding you, the big winners do not try to be fortune tellers.

The correct play here to allow for the unexpected good luck—to allow for more upside—is simply put tight stops immediately below the current price level. If the price falls, the market takes you out. But if you get lucky and the price rises, you ride with it and soon move your stop-loss up to preserve the new lucky profit, too. Since this is so important, the source of so many losses and the subject of so much debate, I'll review.

Ideally, playing for the big money, I'm catching things that are good deals. I'm investing in macroeconomic events; I'm making my play when I believe the rest of the world is wrong, when they're valuing something incorrectly. That's when they sell it cheap because they're down on it and that's the very time I'm going to be able to make a profit, even if I have to wait until later to actually realize that profit.

Let me give you an example. In early July 2009 the world was selling off materials stocks, which were down a lot. I had stops on those, so when they started to go down I sold mine out immediately and took profits on them. As described above, I put those stops on for a particular reason. First I bought those materials stocks, right? I didn't catch them at exactly the right time, but I knew there would be some improvements in the economy (according to my leading indicators).

Everyone around me had been saying, "Whoa, what growth?" They were looking for those green shoots, but they just couldn't see any growth, growth that you now know was already in progress.

They couldn't see it because even though they are famous, and the audience thinks they know what they're talking about, they really just don't know how to calibrate their indicators. I was looking at very early leading indicators that forecast improvement compared to what I saw in those same indicators three months earlier and three months before that. I've never seen a sequence like that where rates of change were improving in sequence like that (or stopped going down as fast) which didn't develop into an actual recovery. The sequence that has never missed is when the six month out indicators turn up, followed by the three month out indicators, followed by coincident improvement, all happening as predicted.

History has already born me out; you can now clearly see the recovery that I forecasted way back in the spring and summer of 2009. Note how much the media were focused on employment, and how little employment really meant in predicting rising profits and an improving economy. You are seeing actual economic growth that most observers were not able to see.

Now I'll make another little prediction just for the fun of it. You will be reading this book in early- to mid-2010. At that point, I'd expect people to be getting pretty optimistic. By the time you read this, I expect that the economy will have actually shown positive growth. In fact, at that point, I believe most American investors will be too confident, and in this I think they will be wrong. The real economic success will be temporary, and the real story will be about the borderless world, not the United States.

My point to all of this is that when I saw that the global economy was going to turn up, and that the world was at that moment selling the materials, I was saying, "I hope they sell a lot." I knew then, and I still believe, that the global economy is going to grow stronger and China is going to be using a lot of copper, and nickel, and zinc and coal. They're going to need all of it. I knew that, sooner or later, the prices of those building blocks of society were going to suddenly get pushed up because I know that during the recession they were not producing much of that stuff so clearly there would not be enough materials around to serve the unexpected spurt of growth.

In my last book, I forecasted just this situation. Everybody knows about the certainty of economic development in Asia, Latin America, and Africa inspired by our western success. The whole world now knows how we live, and nothing will stop the ex-peasants from having at least a middle-class lifestyle.

We know all about this. We've heard about it ad nauseum, but per my forecast, the temporary bout of fear about our own economic downturn has distracted all of us. Typically shortsighted, ignoring the obvious, we didn't stockpile these building blocks of society; we sold our investments in the companies that produce, process, transport, and sell them. There are going to be shortages, the prices are going to soar, and I'm investing in that stuff. Some simple, easy-to-access examples? ETFs: SLX (steel), MOO (agribusiness), XLB (materials), and especially PKOL (coal). Remember you are Investor 2.0. These are ideas to give you a place to start your research, not investment recommendations to a robot who has checked his/her brain at the door.

People don't see all of that right now, as I'm writing this. But if I follow my plan, and the stock prices don't rise on schedule, what happens? Then I buy more! In fact, I may not time it perfectly, I don't really expect to. So what I've done is, I haven't bought all I wanted, I only bought about a third of it, knowing that I'm not going to catch it perfectly, so I buy a third early, and I'll likely buy a bunch more at a better price! The only thing that could possibly change my mind about all of this is if I realize that I was wrong about my expectations for growth in our borderless planetary economy. If that changes, then I obviously wouldn't keep executing that same strategy. If I turn out to be wrong, if my leading indicators don't turn out to mean what I currently think they mean, if positive growth doesn't develop over the autumn and winter of 2009, my strategy will change big time.

For example, if investors around the world catch on faster than I expect, and are totally turned off by the anti-business, anti-global growth policies of our government, I will be much quicker about moving my capital offshore. I will also be much quicker about selling my U.S. real estate holdings, and you should also be ready for a major change in your strategy.

But as long as development around the world continues and the borderless economy continues to be strong, I'm going to keep on investing in those raw materials and building blocks no matter what the market does. Makes sense, right? The reason it makes sense is because I had a strategy involving that.

Again, contrast this story with a technical trade (which I do all the time and have relied on for bread and butter all my life) based on a formation on the charts. I recognize a pattern, and I'm trading it. Then, if it doesn't work right away I'm out, because I know why I made the move. That's the distinguishing thing that determines when you use a price-based stop-loss and when you don't. And by the way, if I think it's gone up enough, and I want to make sure I can take some profits, *then* I'm going to put stops in very close so if the market comes down it takes me out. And as it goes up higher, I keep moving the stops up so I can hold on to those profits.

Rule 2 (Once You Make a Decision, Stick to It)

I mentioned this in passing before, but I want to add emphasis. Whichever way you decide to play it, don't ever change your strategy in mid trade. Don't change from a trade to an investment. Don't chicken out when you've made an investment in value, and when you're making an investment based on a pattern you think you see, don't be afraid to take a loss. You're not obligated to use any particular indicator, but if you do use the indicator, don't rationalize it or make excuses for it. Just let it go, even if you think you're right. Once out of the trade according to plan, you can always buy in again if you have the conviction. But in my experience, even though admitting a mistake is painful, and even though we humans will do everything we can to avoid that moment of truth, once out of a bad trade you will very seldom actually re-enter. You thought you would when you sold out, but once free, you will feel like a whole different person who sees things much differently.

The fact is, since humans are built to lose money and make terrible financial decisions, as we've explained in many parts of this book, it's natural to resist doing whatever is right at the time. For example, let's say I've decided to wait to buy a stock until a huge correction that I expect so I can get a better price. Right on schedule, the stock sells off horribly amid lots of bad news and feeling.

The herd is feeling very negative about that stock and its performance, and as the pathetic herd animal that I am, I just don't feel like buying it either. Ironically, this is true even though I thought the whole thing out in advance, I anticipated the wave of bad feelings, and I was even waiting for it. When the negative crowd reaction comes, exactly as expected, I still don't feel like buying it. I've experienced this reluctance to buy on the expected sell-off, and it can be very intense. That's why I'm not surprised most people lose money, even when (as it turns out) their original idea was right.

In those situations, I've learned from hard experience to discipline myself. I actually say the following to myself as I am saying it to you right now: "This particular time, your instincts may be correct. They certainly feel like it, don't they? And if you follow your plan this time, you'll probably miss out on something. But I know this for certain. The pain of missing out this time is nothing compared to the pain of a life of investing without discipline. If you don't follow your plan now, when will you start?"

By losing tens of millions of dollars and by experiencing gobs of pain, I've learned that changing plans or rationalizing and making excuses for an indicator in the middle of a trade is the kiss of death. Human beings are hard-wired to lose money, and to be terrible at golf. You must do the unnatural to win in either game. That's why I always articulate my plan, put it in writing or have my traders put it in writing, then follow it even when I'm sure I am wrong. I know Chi Chi Rodriguez did, and I'm pretty certain Tiger does too.

Here's an example: I recently had heavy exposure to commodity stocks, particularly agricultural companies such as Monsanto, and to a Platinum ETF. The demand as suggested by our in-house Market X-ray was weak, although with no sellers emerging, the prices rose steadily for more than a month. I know from experience that a rally based on an absence of sellers with little underlying demand is not a lasting one.

I decided in advance that when the number of advancing issues started to thin, I would take profits on those commodity plays before the general markets rolled over, since I didn't want to give up several percentages of gain quickly on a violent correction. That's what I decided in advance, but the stock prices stimulated lots of positive stories in the press and positive feelings in general from investors. It was time to sell, but I just didn't want to. The stocks were still on the way up, after all.

This is how it always is. We humans never feel like following our plan. If making the right investment decision came naturally to investors, there'd be lots of rich people. The country clubs would be packed, and there wouldn't be anyone to cut the grass.

Making the plan is easy. Having the cojones to follow it is another story. That's what separates the hall of famers from the wannabes. I ignored my feelings and sold the stocks when demand started to thin out, although the materials stocks continued a little longer.

I'm not going to recount here how much I saved when a violent correction would have taken much of my profit. That would be poetic, but it isn't the point. The point isn't that I made the move because I could see into the future. If the move turned out to be perfect timing that saved me a bundle of money, then that would be plain dumb luck. The point is I'm a consistently profitable investor because I follow the plan I make when I'm thinking clearly, and I don't change that plan in the heat of battle.

In the Great War, the battle plans were composed in the officers' war room over coffee, not in the heat of battle over adrenaline. I'll remind you again of the story of Ulysses having himself lashed to the mast of his command ship to stop himself from being lured by the Sirens' song. It's a story of achieving greatness by transcending human nature. Knowing he *must* follow his plan, even though every instinct in his body cried out against it. This is how you achieve greatness. There is no other way.

My Bond Strategy for RIGHT NOW

I guess I've become so acclimated to the whole idea of being a broadcaster that I sometimes forget how really connected I've become with my audience. I speak, and you/they hear me right then and there. Radio and television both offer an instantaneous dissemination of information. I get the opportunity to look at the markets every day, and together my audience and I keep up on a day-to-day basis.

Writing a book—well now, this is a little different. If I tell you something about what I did yesterday or today or what I might do tomorrow, it's all based on the markets and economic news that I am able to see as I'm writing this. And of course, I don't have a clue as to when you're reading it. So with all of these disclaimers behind me (and I think I've pretty well covered it), I'd like to pretend you've been right here by my side as I devised and executed my bond strategy.

Here are the conditions as I see them. The administration spent all last year printing money like crazy; the estimates are they printed $12 trillion. Now, when you print $12 trillion, it becomes anything but scarce. And the value of anything goes up and down according to whether it's scarce or plentiful.

What we've been doing is making the dollar too plentiful, far too plentiful. It will therefore eventually fall in value against other currencies; that's automatic. Now this gets just a little more complicated because we are a world not a country. Other dumb countries are printing too much of their currency also, but some countries are managing their affairs with intelligence and forethought.

So the biggest problem I'm facing long term (and the biggest problem you'd be facing today), the thing that we really have to watch out for, is to make sure we don't get caught holding dollars. We don't want our wealth dependent upon the value of the dollar, and we don't want to be confused by the euro, the yen, or the dumb things other countries might do to follow or counter our dumb moves.

Now, let's just consider the United States for a minute, to keep our story simple. The inflation that comes from what we've done already, the already-visible inflation, is a much talked about item. I don't really have to write a book about that. But think about what's really going on behind the scenes.

I listened with interest as the president of the United States talked about his plans, and I know that any way you slice it we're borrowing, one way or the other, many trillions of dollars. So after playing around with a lot of numbers and listening to what everyone is saying about it, I've come up with a number. It's a middle of the road figure of about $5 trillion that we will have borrowed to get ourselves through this period of time. I think that's a fair estimate. If you believe that it's going to be lower, that's fine. I think you're wrong, but you can make the adjustment for yourself.

Lots of you will say it's going to be much higher, and that's fine; I'm just working with a number that I think is very conservative, but we'll end up having borrowed $5 trillion. Now we have a stated goal, and that (according to the president) is that no one who makes less than $250,000 a year is going to pay one penny of extra taxes to help pay back all of this borrowed money. And remember, we're already spending every penny we get our hands on, and so only *new* money will be available to help us pay back the $5 trillion.

So the families who make up one and a half percent of the population (the ones who are in the more-than-$250,000 range) are going to be charged with paying it all back. If you look at that as a 20-year mortgage, that's $5 trillion shared among those people, leaving each one of them owing about a $2 million mortgage! It's simple math, and it means that they'll have about $179,000 a year worth of mortgage payments facing them. Don't forget, they only make $250,000. So, if that isn't going to happen (and clearly it isn't), they won't be paying back principle and interest; they'll be allowing it to compound. Which means that 20 years from now each of these people who has $250,000 income will be responsible for a $7 million loan, or an $800,000-a-year payment!

Any way you slice it, it's going to be impossible to pay it back that way. There's only one way to handle it, and that is to purposely create inflation. You can see what's going to happen to the value of the dollar. Why do I bring all of this to light, just as I'm about to talk to you about bonds? The reason is that bonds are simply about the price of money, and nothing else matters in a bond. It directly relates to the value of the currency that you're going to get paid back in or that you're lending.

So the main factor that determines whether a bond is a good deal or not is the value of what you'll get paid back in. I got involved in the bond market in the first place because I only wanted to take equity risk and make a big bet on the belief that I'd get paid back a lot of money. If I don't have that, I'd just as soon have a nice safe place to *lend* my money.

I mentioned this earlier: We want to invest the way rich people invest, knowing that we deserve a good return on our money. That's the purpose of my strategy to get into bonds. I didn't like the stock market, I didn't like the odds provided by the stock market, and so I decided to be a lender rather than an investor. I know that no matter how tough it is to compete, the one thing all those competitors want is capital.

The people who use cheap labor and work harder and bootleg your software, all those people are surrounded by growing numbers of your competitors, but the one thing they absolutely need is money. How is it that they can look to us for money? Because only in the United States (and to a lesser degree in Western Europe) have we been spending the last half-century creating a surplus.

Everyone else was basically working in the fields; they have no surplus, they need our capital. And they're going to have to pay for it, because there may be plenty of cheap products and plenty of cheap labor in the world all competing, but the global economy is dependent upon one thing and that's having enough working capital.

My strategy is about providing myself with wealth in the future and protecting myself from the purposeful debasement of the dollar. And I believe that those who aren't prepared are going to suffer a sudden decline in wealth that is comparable to, or maybe worse than, September and October of 2008 when the bottom dropped out of the stock market. In this case, I believe the drop is going to be in the value of the U.S. dollar, and I don't want to lose half my wealth, so that's the focus of my long-term strategy. It's not possible for me to invest in something for safety without having this issue of the declining dollar well in hand. You're going to be learning much more about how to play this game, so just turn the page and let's get to it.

10

Demand Top Dollar

The World Needs Your Money—Invest
with the Rich and Famous

In this chapter . . .

- More bonds—shaken, not stirred
- Why we love convertibles
- Fannie, Freddie, Ginny, and me
- Mark it to market
- The rise of interest rates

You Are a Professional Money Manager: The Only Question Is Will You Be a Good One or a Lousy One!

Money is involved in more of your activities every day than anything else. We Americans manage money. That's what we do. And of all of the people in this new world without economic borders, we're the luckiest. For a couple of hundred years, our free market system and the physical blessings of our country have created surplus for us, while the rest of the world was struggling to simply subsist.

The rest of the world has caught on, as we've discussed throughout this book, and they're bound and determined to create for their families the life we've created here in the United States. Those six billion new competitors are creative, courageous, and relentless. They're willing to work long hours for very little pay, as long as it helps lift their families to a level that we here in the United States take for granted.

We can and should compete every step of the way, but there's one thing every one of those competitors needs: capital. There's infinite competition, but not infinite capital. Those adventurous hardworking aspirants all over the globe need your capital to create the lives they've chosen, and they have to pay for it.

I'm a professional investor, and so are you. We both want our money to work for us. When the moment is exactly right, when the deal is weighted enough to my advantage, I love to put my money to work by making equity investments. But I'm here to share the wisdom gained in a lifetime of living by my wits on Wall Street. I understand and you must understand that in this world of infinite opportunity and scarce capital, it is often a better deal to be the lender. Let the other guy take the risk, and let him work for you and me.

Money is fungible. That means all dollars or yen or Yuan or pounds or Euros or kroner or marks are all the same. You can buy the same hamburger and Coke with any of them, and you can use any of them to finance any transaction anywhere on the planet. Money is scarce everywhere, and any currency can be freely changed into any other currency.

Somebody asked me if he shouldn't be afraid to buy a Chinese bond. There's no such thing as a Chinese bond, because they're the same as American bonds. If the currency of one country is at risk, the interest rate in that country will rise to account for that. Bonds are bonds are bonds. People and businesses around the world need your capital and they're willing to pay for it in any currency or any denomination.

If money is needed for development in one country and people or businesses are willing to pay more to borrow it, money will begin to flow to that country. When that happens, borrowers in other countries will have to offer more. Rates will be forced up everywhere. The only way money can be plentiful on one side of a border and scarce on the other side, is if property rights are protected on one side and not the other. This is why money has traditionally flowed to the United States from everywhere else.

Today, other countries have realized that to attract capital they must improve the conditions, and at the same time we in the United States seem intent on moving our policies in the opposite direction. It's time for you to understand the largest and most powerful of all financial markets: the bond market. You can now be a *lender* in a world without boundaries.

Relationships (between Stocks and Bonds)

I was doing my radio program the other day, and Shannon called to ask about an article she read. It was about the relationship between stocks and bonds. Essentially she read that conventional wisdom tells us that if stocks go up, bonds go down and vice versa. This is what she *told* me she read: "Treasury yields rising should be bad for equities, but so far this year, 10-year bond yields and stock prices have basically been in lock step." Well Shannon, let's clear things up. On one hand you're talking about bonds going up, and on the other you're indicating bond yields. It's not the same. Bond prices and bond yields go in *opposite* directions, so it's either one or the other that's moving.

I can't tell you how many people over the years have told me they had so much trouble grasping this one concept that they gave up on the bond market completely. They just decided it was too complicated for them. But I know what you meant, Shannon. Let's straighten this out once and for all, and when you get how simple it is and how familiar these ideas already are to you in your daily life, you may never be intimidated by a financial instrument again.

The Rent's Not Free, But It's on the House

Money feels so abstract to some people. They have a tough time grasping concepts that come naturally in other areas of their lives. When you see how simple this is, you're going to understand bonds much better, because I'm going to compare them to something that you already understand. You understand rent, right? Well, interest is simply the price you pay to rent some money. When you need some money, you can either go into your big walk-in vault, where you keep tons of it lying around, or you can choose to rent some. You rent money exactly the same way you rent a house, but people seem to comprehend that concept so much more easily when it's in reference to the house. I'll show you that it's the same thing.

Let's say you own a house, you paid maybe a $100,000 for it, and you'd like to rent it out. The problem is there are way too many vacancies out there. Rents are running pretty cheap in that area. Now, ask yourself this question: When the rents are running cheap, do you think a potential renter wants a long-term lease or a short-term lease? Obviously he wants to lock in that cheap rent for as long as possible, right? As the landlord, you want a really short-term lease. After all, rents may go up around there, and you'll want to be free to renegotiate. So now you at least understand the motivation of both sides.

Moving along, let's assume you've found a very reliable tenant. And you don't want to even *think* about that place being empty. So you've made a deal with the guy for a long-term 10-year lease. You won't have to worry about vacancies for sure. But let's cut to a few years into this thing. The economy is on the rise, things are rosier, and rents are moving up—in fact other houses in your neighborhood are renting for quite a bit more than the house you own. You're getting $10,000 a year, and your fellow landlords are getting as much as $15,000 a year. And you're still locked in until the completion of that 10-year lease.

Remember, you paid about a hundred grand for the house, and you're locked in to a long-term lease deal. After a little thought, you decide maybe you'll just get out of this thing, and you're ready to sell. With the help of the classifieds or maybe a little ad on Craig's List, you've found a buyer! Now the buyer wants to know one thing: "Is there anything in particular you'd like to disclose to me before we agree on this deal?" And you reply, "Well actually, the place is in great shape, and everything is as it seems. The only thing is I've got about another seven years left on this lease deal I signed with the current tenant. But look, I'm getting around ten grand a year for the place!"

Your prospective buyer is now giving you a look. He says out loud what he's thinking inside. "Hold it. I can get $15,000 a year on any of these other houses around here, but I'm only going to get 10 if I buy yours? The rest of these places are available at around a hundred grand, but hey I'm sorry. I'll tell you what, how about I give you seventy grand?"

The analysis: You still have the same house you had before, the same house everybody else has. In fact, you're still getting the same rent you were before, the same ten grand. But because all the other rents went up, the value of your house fell. All along, the actual value of your house was dependent on the rents in the neighborhood around you. Of course, if the rents in the neighborhood had gone down during this same period, then the value of your house obviously would have gone up, thanks to the fact that you'd locked in a nice long-term lease at ten grand a year.

The rent that folks are paying around you is a major factor in determining the value of your house. That $10,000 annually is called the *yield*, and if folks around you are getting 15, that makes your house worth about $70,000 (that's called the *current yield*). But you're thinking, "Whoa, wait a minute. If I sell the house for $70,000, and that tenant moves out, then the rent's going to go up. That'll make the house worth a hundred grand again."

The buyer's a reasonable guy. He says, "OK, you're right; it's only worth seventy today because of the rent situation. I'll give you eighty for it, because I know the value will eventually catch up to the other houses." Now (in the bond market) that's called the yield-to-maturity. Because even though you've locked in a comparatively low rent and the price of the bond has gone down, eventually the bond is going to mature at the original price. So you factor that in when you figure the yield-to-maturity.

Renting money via a bond is the same as renting a house. Interest is the same as rent. If the rates around you go up and you've locked in the old rate, then the value of your house or your bond is pushed down, and vice versa. If the rates go down, the value is pushed up. It may seem elementary, but looking at it this way should help you to understand better, and, as you know, knowledge and information can make you rich.

Interest Rates and Stock Prices

Now how do interest rates relate to stock prices? It's also common sense—no memorization, just understanding things you're already familiar with in your personal life. (You just didn't know how much you already knew.)

Lower interest rates mean that a company will pay less to borrow money, so the company automatically makes more profit. It means that its customers have to pay less to buy the products, and that helps sales. It means that alternate investments (like putting money in the bank) pay less. When that happens it makes the stocks more attractive. Those things together are overwhelming, and very often when interest rates rise, stocks go down, and vice versa. Now, watch this.

Sometimes what happens as the economy starts to improve a little bit, and as we get a few transactions going, interest rates start to rise. That's simply because people are taking out loans; they're out there actually doing something with the money. And by the way, I'm not talking about one-day interest rates; we're talking now about 5-, 10-, 15-, and 20-year interest rates. So the interest rates rise a little bit from the death spiral they've been in.

In this case, as interest rates rise the stock market also rises because the strength of the economy is helping both of them. It's easy to see if you realize these things are *not* tied together with steel; they're tied together with rubber bands. They move together, but there's flexibility. And you can make generalizations, but there will always be times when things are backwards. Like when people get really scared, like they did back in September 2008. At moments of extreme fear interest rates fall and stocks go down at the same time. That's because in extreme cases the rules don't apply. People do whatever they feel in panic.

Dinosaurs and Bonds

Rehashing that radio call from Shannon just reminded me that we haven't really talked about bonds that much. So let's do. The story about bonds isn't really about bonds, it's about dynamic thinking. Let me simplify that, it's about *flexible* thinking, the ability to adapt to your environment. Dinosaurs couldn't adapt, and you remember what happened to them, right? But human beings have been able to adapt beautifully. Now the question is, can you adapt to your social and cultural environment?

This chapter will give you a whole new route to the life you want—a whole new way to look at money and investing. Well, OK, not really new; this is mostly common sense and mostly things you already understand, just as you already understood about the rents versus house prices.

In reality, the richest people, governments, and companies on Earth have for centuries been relying on what you're about to learn. Even today, 90 percent of all the money in the world is invested by lending (and with guaranteed returns) in the bond market. The companies that send salesmen to sell you stocks and mutual funds actually rely on the bond market for most of their money. You see, bonds are not often meant to be traded, so they don't generate enough transactions for the retail brokerage business. A bond can earn you interest for years, and you don't have to do anything but collect the money. But the bond doesn't do anything for the people who want to sell you investments. If you aren't going to be buying and selling it, they're not anxious to introduce it to you.

To me bonds make for interesting conversation. I'd like to have a dollar for every investor who's said to me, "I sure wish there was a place to learn about bonds. Hey Dan! How about a book about bonds?" Folks, it isn't going to take a book. The subject is much simpler than that. Basically, a bond is a promise, any promise. You're used to stocks, because that's what your advisors have preferred to sell you on. Besides, stocks make a much more interesting *media story*.

The thing that makes stocks *so interesting* is they're a zero-sum gain. The stock market is built on uncertainty. It exists *because* of uncertainty. Money is invested in the stock market by someone who thinks that what he's investing in is going up. He's buying that investment from someone who thinks it's going down. He's buying it from somebody who thinks that it's worth *less* than what he's getting for it, so it's a zero-sum gain.

In the stock market, *some*body has to be wrong, either the buyer or the seller. You can see how this generates the thrill of victory, the agony of defeat, the postgame wrap up, the pregame analysis. The stock market is a *natural* for media coverage. And that boring old bond market is, by contrast, much like a late-night program on cable called "Watching Your Grass Grow."

The bond market is based on *certainty*. As the deal is made, somebody is lending money with the certainty that they're going to get it back. The time and the amount of principle that's being lent, and the amount that's coming back, and the price of the money (the interest) is already set in advance. Both parties know exactly how the deal will come out. If either of them doesn't like the deal, it doesn't get done.

Again, that's the opposite of the stock market. The reason it's so difficult to find information about the bond market is that there *isn't* any specific information. But the basics remain simple: Any kind of deal where you promise to give something, get a promise of receiving something, and where both sides understand the deal in advance, that's a bond.

Here's where it gets creative. The way the bond is configured can be anything that the human mind can imagine. It can be a discount, where the principle is paid at the end and the interest is essentially being paid because you're getting back more principle than you put in. That's a zero-coupon bond. It can be set up like a typical corporate bond or most Treasuries. That's generally where you get interest only, and then the principle is paid back at the end.

You can have the interest paid weekly, monthly, or yearly. You can have the interest stepping up gradually over time, or adjustable and calculated according to an index or according to how something in the marketplace goes; any promise where you use my resources and then you pay me back, with the conditions preset and agreed upon is a bond. And that's why there's no information. It's simply all about the skill of calculating, designing, and negotiating what the deal is going to be. Generally speaking, it has to be a win-win situation to happen, because both sides know how the deal ends.

Elsewhere in this book I discuss how I focused in on bonds in 2001. It was sort of by default really, because I knew the stock market was going to get pretty tough, but I also knew people would continue to compete and that they'd be forced to pay a premium for scarce capital. Businesses may not have room for much profit margin, but if they want to stay in business, they have to have the capital to function. The owners of the businesses may have a rough time making a profit, but the lenders have to be paid first. And the bond business, as you now know, is about lending money.

I've defined a bond for you in a variety of ways. How about this? A bond is a deal that gets a loan for the person or company who wants to benefit now and pay later. That's one side. On the other side, it promises to make enough profit for the lender to make him want to do the deal. You pay for life insurance because you like the death benefit compared to the premium, so life insurance is one kind of a bond. Here's another: You take an employment contract and willingly come to work all week long in order to receive a payment on Friday and a pension contribution and benefits.

So, you lend money to a company or financial institution because you like the terms—what they're going to pay you to use your money (the interest)—and they borrow the money because they think there's enough room for them to profit from using it.

Here's a part people have trouble grasping. You're accustomed to making investments with the goal of earning capital gains. Every day people buy and sell shares in the public markets, and every day the prices are recorded. If the prices go up, you've gained, and if they go down, you've lost. But what if there isn't any trade? How much has your house value gone up or down today?

What about a bond that represents a loan from one person to another—a deal designed to earn interest for years? Since nobody planned on selling the contract, there isn't an exchange to buy and sell it. It just isn't meant to trade. If you were to try to calculate a price for it at any given time, the price would just be a matter of opinion.

Our country, in one of the biggest financial blunders in history, paralyzed its economy and put our most important financial institutions virtually out of business by insisting on assigning arbitrary values to bonds that had no mechanism for valuation. In their ignorance, our regulators were trying to apply stock valuation methods to illiquid promises.

Ask yourself about the value of your promise to support your family, clean your garage, or show up on time for work? The promises are not valueless, but the value at any given moment is totally subjective until you actually do what you promise. If these same promises were traded daily on an exchange, it would be meaningful and easy to assign daily values to them.

Ironically most of the mortgage bonds that were the center of this almost lethal controversy never stopped paying interest and are still in force today.

The board in charge of our federal accounting standards simply stopped insisting on using the incalculable daily prices as a measure of solvency for the banks in question, and the entire problem disappeared. Note that very little of the hundreds of billions of dollars foolishly assigned by two different administrations was used. When the accounting standards were modified the problem disappeared.

Understand that the concept of judging these promises according to an arbitrary daily or monthly valuation is not strategically helpful in evaluating bonds in the account of a bank, a brokerage firm, or in *your* account. This is where all the confusion comes from, and it can best be dealt with by completely ignoring the issue.

You miss out on being able to use some of the safest and most powerful financial tools ever invented by trying to fit them into your preconceived investment notions.

I recommend that you consider applying the concept of the tipping point, which is much more applicable. Conditions move in an expected direction incrementally over time, and the markets suddenly catch up all at once. This is how it happens. The reasons bonds are a safer instrument for such a strategy is because they provide for guaranteed return of principle (with interest) regardless of whether we get our strategy right. They only have to stay in business in order to pay us back.

When we buy bonds from a company—that is, when we lend money to a company—we underwrite using a different set of standards than we would if we were actually investing and taking equity. Here, all we really need to ascertain is that the borrower has the willingness and the ability to repay; the borrower or issuer doesn't necessarily have to be the best company in the industry or anything like that.

Get this straight and you've got the whole idea. The bonds mature at par. This means you get back the promised amount of money at the known maturity date. As long as you're happy with the interest and principle you're guaranteed to receive, why do you care how some strangers value the bond in the meantime?

You only have to be satisfied that the borrower has the willingness and ability to repay the loan. To judge the ability of a company to service its debt, you can study the company's balance sheet—sometimes you can actually speak to the people at the company itself, but there's a shortcut. It's very accurate in fact; it's the way banks do it.

There's an NYU professor named Altman who issues something called the Z-Scores. They're published in a lot of different places, Bloomberg among them. And we've found those Altman Z-Scores to be very useful—much more so than the Standard and Poor's or Moody's ratings that have gotten so many bond buyers into trouble.

They are *only* about solvency and the ability to repay bonds. They are *not* about extraneous details, and they're not based on the size of the company. Altman doesn't accept offers to "go to lunch," and the companies don't pay for his ratings, as they do with Moody's and S&P. And those two have proven to be anything but reliable.

There's an additional benefit of these bonds. You already know the bonds generate revenue, paid to us for the use of our money, and you already know the bonds can be held to maturity, where we're guaranteed to get $1,000 a bond—as long as the borrowing company stays in business. But the bonds can also be sold early if our strategy works early and the bond price goes up.

Let me give you an example of how corporate bonds have made my life easier and safer. Many investors bought Cisco Systems stock in the $70s and ended up selling it in a panic for less than $10 per share! Clearly, if the Cisco Systems stock was going to mature at $70 in a few years, nobody would ever have sold it for $9 and change. Because bonds have a predetermined outcome, they can provide a level of certainty of results that cannot be obtained by instruments that do not have that maturity.

The example above shows precisely why buying a bond fund is not the same as buying a bond. Sure, a bond fund has a bunch of bonds in it, but the bond fund itself does not mature; it continually keeps getting rolled over. So they've taken a bunch of safe instruments and made them into a risky instrument by putting them into an ongoing portfolio. Again, because a bond has a predetermined outcome—that is, it's going to mature at $1,000—it can provide a level of certainty that cannot be obtained by instruments that don't mature at a fixed price, like stocks or even bond mutual funds.

You know I actually learned about the bond market out of necessity, and I learned about it very late in life, but the minute I did my life improved, my results picked up, and—lo and behold!—I made more money in the stock market because of bonds. Once I had this certainty option, and was already earning assured profits, I could afford to be choosy about where I took stock market risk, and which uncertainties I placed bets on. I could cherry pick my risk positions and increase my odds of winning. I'm absolutely positive that you, too, will do better in all of your investments—stocks, commodities, metals, real estate— if you understand bonds.

As we've said many times in this book, the very, very rich who control most of the money know that their money belongs in their pocket. Throughout the book, I've pointed out certain things that I said I really want you to get. Well here's one for sure: Your money belongs in your pocket. The only reason for you to invest your money and take risks is because you have a real conviction that you're going to get back much more money than you put in. Otherwise you can lend your money out to a safe place where you know you'll get it back *and* get paid well for its use, especially in a scarce capital environment like we have right now.

More on Bonds

I knew it. I knew if I got started on a discussion about bonds, it'd be hard to stop. This is about the aforementioned opportunities. It's about how the real guys—the great investors—have enough confidence to know they're going to get theirs. I can hear you saying it now, that it seems like the rich people get all the opportunities. But really, they just know how to react when the opportunities present themselves.

This part about rich people keeping their money in their pockets, it came from my grandfather. He was a very wise old owl, and you've heard me talk about him before. Here's a quote I've been passing on to people forever. He said. "Rich people don't feel any pressure to be invested all the time; they don't feel an obligation to constantly do deals." They know that the only time they should take their money out of their pockets is when they have something very compelling to invest in. Then maybe they'll take some risks. Otherwise, they *lend* their money out and get paid first by the people who need the capital.

So I say it again: The real guys have got enough confidence to know that their opportunity for a good play is going to come. The great champions in boxing don't constantly run in there swinging wildly. The great football coaches don't go for it on fourth down in the second quarter, and they rarely go for it on fourth down at all even if they think they can make it, even if their quarterback is begging them to let him go, even if he's *sure* he can make it. If the team is in the wrong place on the field, and they have more to lose than to gain, the seasoned professional coach is just not going to take the chance. And you know why: because he realizes that the risk outweighs the reward.

I avoid risk the same way those great players do. And I don't go for it in the stock market when the herd is stampeding in panic.

I Was Too Dumb to Be Interested in Bonds . . .

In 2001 I realized something. Here I was at 56 years old, and the only thing I'd ever made any money on in my entire life was stocks and commodities. If fact, I'd made a *lot* of money on those fluctuating, risky investments, right up through the '90s. And then suddenly I realized the situation had totally changed. As I explained earlier, I could see the profit margins disappearing as the world became a much more competitive place, and we were on a much more level playing field than ever before.

My newest realization was, "Why would I want to risk the money that I won in the '90s? Why would I want to risk that money investing in companies that are in such a competitive environment? They *all* know how to do the same stuff, and the profit margins are diminished to near zero!"

I mean, think about Best Buy! How much margin are they getting by selling those fabulous computers? One percent? Two percent? Five percent? This stuff is made by people all around the world willing to work and make just enough to pay their help, never mind profitability. So who would want to invest and risk money in an environment like that? You? Well, certainly not me! So stocks were a bad deal, and it looked for the foreseeable future that they'd stay that way. And by the way dear reader, here we are in 2009 with the realization that this was in fact a correct assessment.

Some of my old Wall Street friends that I'd known as a young man had gone into the bond business, and when I looked them up, I found that these guys always make money in every type of environment. There's always a deal for them because they can always structure *something*. Whether it's on the way up or on the way down, people always need money. And just between you and me, some of these guys had never really seemed to me like the sharpest tools in the shed, yet they were able to find profitable niches.

So I remembered another piece of my grandfather's advice. Something he told me when I was a preteen. He said Americans think that anything they don't understand is risky, and of course, they're right; it is risky to do things you don't understand. But they also don't want to study beyond a certain age. They have this illusion that they're grown up and finished studying.

Since they think that everything they don't understand is risky, and since they don't really want to understand anything new, you can often find deals where you can get paid as though you took a lot of risk, and all you *really* did was your homework! What a deal—I get paid for making a highly risky bet, when all I did was read the fine print and pick out the bet that wasn't really that risky. That's what the bond market has been for me, and it can be the same for you.

Convertible Bonds (More Arrows in My Quiver)

When the market's throwing curve balls, as it seems destined to do for the rest of my days, I always feel a lot more comfortable knowing I've got a good variety of weaponry, lots of different kinds of arrows in my quiver, lots of different tools in my tool belt—pick your metaphor. When I have all of these choices at my disposal, I'm not stuck having to buy stocks all the time because I'm under pressure to make money right away or because I'm worried about when I'm going to retire.

This is another device that enables me to wait for my moment in the stock market, and take risk *only* when I know I'm going to get paid a lot. When the moment or the opportunity is not close enough to perfect, I can choose tools in which my outcome is much more certain. Like the very rich, I insist on actually getting paid for the use of my money. Convertible bonds are really a hybrid strategy, and there's a particular time when a convertible bond makes a wonderful tool. These bonds are often way too cheap for the value they offer because even many pros are afraid of convertible bonds.

And you know what they're afraid of? Complexity. People avoid these bonds because they think convertibles are too complex. Now, it's true you have to think of a couple of things at the same time. You get interest, and you get the right to convert this into a stock whenever you want. That way, if the company doesn't absolutely kill, you're still getting paid interest, and you have the safety of a maturity date, a certain date when you actually get your money back.

You should bear in mind that no matter how much you like a stock, it never matures. There's no date when you get back the full amount you invested. You're always dependent on the market price. If you own a stock and the market is wrong and stays that way for a long time, you're still out of luck.

Investors often make the mistake of confusing preferred stocks with bonds. Actually, preferred stocks have many of the same weaknesses as their common brothers. A preferred stock does earn income, but you never have a certain date to get your money back—preferred stocks generally don't mature. You're always at risk because the changing value of the preferred stock can always cause you to lose money. What good are all those dividends if you take a huge permanent hit on the price of the preferred stock?

But a convertible bond, like any bond, will mature at a certain time. So you know that as long as the issuing company doesn't go out of business, you're going to get your money back on a certain date. You don't have that enormous risk to principle that you have on any equity investment. And if the company *does* do what it's supposed to do, you'll get to convert your investment into a stock—at your demand and with your timing, with the benefits of hindsight! You get to benefit just as the stockholders do.

Now, I think people are afraid of these things because they're intimidated and some are even a little lazy. The complexity that turns many investors off is exactly what makes these instruments very attractive to those of us who are looking for an opportunity to do a little homework and get paid as though we were taking a lot of risk. Convertible bonds can offer you more than just the interest, but you have to calculate whether it's a good deal, and then you also have the right to convert, so you have to evaluate that option. I know. It's a *little* complex. But not liking a convertible bond because of its complexity is like saying, "I don't like sundaes; there's the ice cream and the syrup, the nuts, the cherry. It's all too confusing." That's silly!

You seem to have no trouble at all driving while reading road signs, changing lanes, changing the radio station *and* combing your hair at the same time; you can even simultaneously relive that last argument you were having with your spouse. You have the ability to juggle all these things in your mind with all of those "complexities." You say you can't handle complexity? I say, "Get over it." These are extremely powerful tools. They've made me tremendous money several times in my life when nothing else would work.

The real truth is, in the tough times that we're in right now, I'd be ahead of the game if I had in the last 20 years done absolutely nothing except invest in convertible bonds once every five years and then take my profit. I would have been better off than almost everyone who's been working at this for the last 20 years—most of whom have ended up with nothing.

Personally, I like the odds of success with the right convertible bond, issued by a company with a great Asia/global growth strategy, over the common stocks of some of the giants who were big winners in the 1990s.

Convertible Bonds: The Real Nuts and Bolts

OK. Now that you're past the intimidation, let's talk about exactly what a convertible bond is and think about how the idea might have been conceived. Let's say a guy has a great idea, he's come up with a great new widget or new product of some kind. He's very excited about it, and he's ready to get out there and get rich. The only problem is, like anyone else, he's going to need some capital to grow and execute. He needs to borrow some money. So he goes out into the world and begins to explain his idea to various people, and the following is the essence of virtually every response he hears.

"You know, that's a very good idea. But the problem is it's risky. I don't know if you're gonna succeed or fail. And if you succeed, even if you're paying me a high rate of interest like 9 or 10 percent, that high rate of interest is only gonna contribute to your failure; it's hard to run a business with those high interest rates. And even if you do succeed and pay me back, heck, I was the one taking the risk.

I get back nine or 10 percent, sure, but *you* get rich, and I took all of the risk, And if you fail I get *nothing*? No, no, I don't think so."

It's tough for a guy with a new business, right? No matter how good his idea is, it's hard to get the money. Well, what about this? What if we add in a little "equity kicker"? In other words, I'll lend you the money, but if you succeed, I also get a big sweetener. I'm going to get an option that says even though the stockholders were just sitting around receiving no interest or dividends, I was collecting interest. And if and when you succeed, I'll actually be able to convert my bond into a stock and begin to benefit from the rising stock price and the profits, just as the stockholders do.

Now it becomes a pretty sweet deal, but it's still not sweet enough for me. You see, as nice as the upside is, I still can't get past the fact that the company could easily fail, and I could be the big loser. I'm sorry, but at the point when that new company is making that offer it's too early in his business life cycle for me. I've seen too many promising businesses fail. No matter how profitable it *might* be, I'm not interested in taking a risk on a startup like that.

But here we are three or four years later, and the bond that was issued way back at the beginning of the life of the company is still in existence. And while it's true that some of those companies have disappeared from the face of the Earth (and the people who lent them money have lost their money), some of those companies have actually succeeded. Some in fact have become very successful, and yet those old bonds are still out there.

For a company that issued a bond with high yield and the right to convert during a normal economy and then found success, well, to be honest you're not really going to be able to get a good deal on that one, because the market has adjusted for it and the price of the bond is very high. You won't get much yield now that the outcome is more certain.

But every few years you run into an economic scare. People get worried about the economy and overly concerned, and sometimes that concern turns to outright panic. At that point we have what we call a "flight to quality." And if you don't know what that means, I'll enlighten you. It means they've completely lost their minds, and they're not willing to do anything except lend money to the U.S. government. (Remember the government has the ability to print money, so they're sure they're going to get their money back no matter what; they think they're eliminating risk.)

This knee-jerk panic reaction is wrong for many reasons, not the least of which is the fact that they're buying those Treasuries at very high prices, and are almost sure to lose money unless they hold the Treasuries all the way to maturity. As they hold the bonds to maturity, they have their money tied up at very low interest for years.

In any case, during those panics nobody will touch these convertible bonds. They're still in the high-yield category, and the spread between corporate bonds and Treasuries gets very, very wide. You now have a bond that was issued by a company that's done well and the bond may have a 5 or 6 percent yield, but because there are some people who have to sell these bonds—maybe they need the money to pay their taxes or something—whatever it is, they have to sell them. And guess what? There's nobody to buy them.

While you can't generally find *hundreds* of millions of dollars worth of these bonds, you can buy a *couple* of million dollars worth of them or even a few thousand dollars worth. And at these panic moments, these flights to quality, you can buy them at a gigantic discount, sometimes 60 or 70 cents on the dollar. Again, the reason for that is there are just no buyers for it, and if the guy has to sell it he's sometimes forced to take whatever price he can get. I think it's worth it to examine these numbers a little more closely. Let's do.

If you have a bond that pays, let's say, 6 percent, that's a modest interest rate. But, if you buy that bond for 60 cents on the dollar, you didn't really put a $1,000 into it; you only put $600, right? So if you bought it for $600 and it's paying $60 a year in interest, you're collecting a 10 percent current yield. And it gets even better than that because that bond will mature in a couple of years. And when it does, not only will you have received your interest, but even if nothing great happens with that company—even if it just stays in business—you get back a $1,000 dollars for every $600 you put in. You're going to get *another 40 percent* over a couple of years!

In fact if the stock does well it may be that you not only collect that high rate of interest, you convert the bond into a common stock and benefit along with the other stockholders. It's a beautiful story. But in reality, you know what would have been more likely to happen? People wouldn't have touched that bond because they were engaged in a panic flight to quality. They had blinders on, and all they could see were those Treasuries.

At least that's the way they act at home as regular folks, where they're just a consumer, a typical member of the herd, and where they act irrationally. That same person that we're describing is probably far more rational in the way he conducts business at the office, but here he's in a completely different frame of mind. So he's willing to provide commercial credit to an oil drilling company and grant $60,000 or $100,000 a month of commercial credit because that company has a good name, and he feels very comfortable. On the other hand, when he comes home he's in a completely different mode. Now he's watching television, he's in this panic mode, and he's not willing to buy a bond issued by that same driller. At that moment, that consumer only trusts the U.S. government, and for that he's settling for maybe 2 or 3 percent interest.

So one day the guy wakes up and realizes that the economy is going to survive and that the U.S. government will exist for another few years. He realizes that he's been willing to grant commercial credit to a company, but he wasn't willing to buy their bonds. He's granting commercial credit at the office, while at home he's accepting 2 percent from the government, and he finally asks himself, "Am I out of my mind?"

He cashes in the Treasuries and buys the convertible bond issued by a company that he's perfectly willing to do business with and grant credit to, and as soon as he does that—hello—everybody else does it too. That's right; they've all come to that conclusion at roughly the same time. And when they do, that convertible bond issued by the driller will go up in value right away, and it'll quickly be priced near par—near $1,000 a bond or even above it—long before the bond matures. And so it's possible to make very high rates of return in a year or two because when the panic subsides those bonds always go back to normal.

I can tell you that I've done this at the end of every recession in the past two decades, and here's a little secret for you: Long before the stock market is ready to actually become a bull market and move up, the convertible bonds actually begin to move up first. People wake up to the idea of convertible bonds before they're ready to start investing in stocks.

So not only is this an early way to make money and a strategy that will work when other strategies don't work, but it's also a very good indicator or clue to the market. Once you see the convertible bond prices moving up, it's time to start doing your medium- to long-term equity plays as well.

CHAPTER

11

Now You Have the Power

Create the Results You Want! Earnings Season

In this chapter...

- The Blackstone story
- Cavemen don't get rich
- Making money—The opposite of human nature
- Danger—A final warning

Common Sense and Fundamentals

Earnings season is that period of time during which a large number of publicly traded companies release their quarterly earnings reports. On one of my recent radio shows, I was discussing how futile it is to follow (and bet on) earnings season when you hear those reports on TV. So this listener sends me an email.

She says, "I heard your show today and you said that stocks shouldn't be picked based on fundamentals, but I must have missed a part. If stocks shouldn't be chosen based on fundamentals, if nobody can see the future, then what criteria am I supposed to use to pick a particular stock—just the trend?" And it's signed, "Regards, Judy."

Well, there's no denying that some people have been very successful investing money based on a fundamental story. John Rutledge, a great friend of mine, is one of them. Mario Gabelli does it very effectively. Frank Cappiello and John Dessauer, both those guys also

175

invest based on commonsense economics and fundamentals, as well as my friend and mentor, Dr. Arthur Laffer, he does it too and does it beautifully.

In my experience there are a few necessary conditions that allow this to work for these guys. For me, I have to have really intimate knowledge of a company; it helps if I have some say in the management. Gabelli gets involved with the boards of many of the companies he invests in. But generally speaking, most people don't really know very much about the companies they invest in at all. They do it through mutual funds because they hear about the company; they see the CEO on television a little bit, they get an impression. They don't have the depth of knowledge about these companies, as do the giants I've just mentioned.

Then again, Dr. John Rutledge is really sort of a different case. John is so well established, so well respected, and so famous that he can afford to wait a couple of years to be right. He has tremendous conviction and confidence in his analysis, and the people who hire him—princes, governments, billionaires—also have confidence in his analysis. It works for John; they don't fire him. And I know him very well; he doesn't just sit back and wait. John is constantly going over his ideas to make sure he still agrees with them, to make sure all his suppositions are still there. When he does, he's got the courage to wait for the inevitable, and this has made John Rutledge a rich man. If you can do it the way he does it, I recommend it highly.

Now, you don't often hear me giving specific stock tips or stock advice, and I certainly couldn't do it in a book. If the sky falls tomorrow, that might just change things a bit. But talking about John Rutledge has inspired me to show you somewhat of a John Rutledge-esque sort of idea. It's based on the spread between what people think and reality (which is what they're *going* to think later). You can call it a stock tip. I'll call it The Blackstone Story.

The Blackstone Story

In the summer of 2009, when I was writing this chapter, U.S. financial companies were (in general) probably the most hated, feared, reviled group of companies on the planet. And it's at just that moment that they may have become really good deals; in fact, forget the word "may," I think they *did*. It's worth your time to study up on The Blackstone Group. The guys who run this company are and always have been the smartest guys in the room no matter what room they're in. And whether the day you read this book is the exact right day for you to invest in that company or not, I suggest you get to understand the Blackstone story. I also suggest that you learn enough about it so that you can buy and sell Blackstone several times during the rest of your life.

This year, I'm liking Blackstone even more than usual, with the following caveat: The rest of the market tries to play against CEO Schwartzman and Blackstone management instead of with them. This is a big mistake. See, Blackstone went public at the very top of the euphoric merger and acquisition market of 2007. They sold much of the company for nearly $8 billion just as the celebrations of record stock prices were going on, and just as all the experts were leading their followers to believe it would go on forever.

Blackstone has always been unbelievably adept at buying companies cheap, taking them private, removing the foolish public market pressures from the CEOs and management, making those companies whole and effective and more productive, and then selling them into the market at huge profits. They've done this over and over and over. These guys are very smart. They have the absolute confidence of sovereign wealth funds around the globe, as well as some of the world's richest and smartest people.

So after selling to the public around 40 at every top tick, the stock sold off consistently for a good year and a half in the hands of the people who bought from Blackstone. It finally got down into the low single digits, where it was worth maybe a couple of billion dollars. Blackstone lives in a target-rich environment, so while there are many bargain companies out there that can't get money to operate and grow, Blackstone has shown they can get the money to do pretty much whatever they want.

Now, a new mistake by the market creates an opening for us. The stock just took a 20 percent hit based on a news story. The story says the FDIC wants to make it tougher for private equity firms like Blackstone to take over banks. The FDIC is afraid that these guys will use too much leverage, borrow too much money, and that they'll turn the companies around and sell out too soon, leaving the banks vulnerable. This is capitalism. They should be *allowed* to do that, but the way our government is now being run during this current economy, well, it's making rule changes to prevent this kind of business from happening.

But that's not the end of it; there's more to the story.

The Rest of the Story

Now, the FDIC needs guys like Blackstone to help strengthen the banking system. But in their ignorance, this government agency is proposing rules that actually make it harder and less profitable for Blackstone to work its magic on the banks. The market is making a big mistake. See, the banks need Blackstone more than Blackstone needs the banks. Blackstone can make a fortune on companies in any industry it wants to. It can do its business in China and India if it wants to. And if it wants to acquire banks and we make the rules unattractive, that is exactly what they will do.

So *now* look what's going to happen. You're going to end up with the smartest people (with the most money) moving over and helping to grow the banking system of the countries we're going to be competing with. Listen, on the scale that Blackstone operates on and with their contacts, they can make private deals with the Chinese government, with the premier of China or anybody they want. They have the cooperation of sovereign wealth funds; they can get their cooperation in any deal they want.

I'm no more afraid that these bad decisions in the United States are gonna hurt Blackstone than I am that the head of the Little League is gonna damage Major League Baseball. It *ain't* gonna happen. And based on that opinion, I say Blackstone is a stock you can learn about, get confidence in, and buy and sell several times in your life. Whether the market falls too in love or gets too panicked—at either extreme the market will be wrong because Blackstone is just gonna keep rolling along, basically ignoring the market and the government and the regulators. Remember, these are the smartest guys in the room.

Now for me, I frankly don't want to fit into my life the pain of being on the losing side of an investment for months or years. For me, life is too short. I don't have that lifetime of adulation to fall back on, so I have to be right faster than the giants I mentioned before.

My observation of most people is they don't have the courage to stay with something through thick and thin, especially when they don't know that much about it and they don't have the conviction.

They tend to get involved in deals they haven't really thought through well enough. They think they're going by fundamentals, but they're really going by someone else's idea that they just happened to over-hear. It probably sounded logical so they committed to it, and then it goes in the wrong direction. Inside they know they really didn't do the work, and consequently they run out of gas, they run out of strength. They give up and sell, often at the bottom.

Earlier in the book I told you about an interview I did some years ago with the great champion boxer Jesse James Leija. This conversation meant a lot to me personally, and in some ways it was a game changer for me. Let me bring it up again here, because it helps me illustrate my point.

James unfortunately had the bad luck to be peaking in his career just as Oscar De La Hoya came onto the scene. So I said to James, "Here I am watching the eighth round and here's the great Jesse James Leija, a boxer who's spent his entire life starving and getting hit over and over. He's done everything necessary to get himself on nationwide television. He's on pay-per-view; he's being watched by hundreds of millions of people. This is a culmination of his life's work. I'm sitting here watching the fight in the eighth round, and the announcer says it looks like the guy's getting tired. He's getting tired? James! How is it possible for a guy to get tired at that moment? He's in the eighth round and he can't make it for 12 more minutes—with rest periods?"

Leija looked at me and said, "You know, Dan, the fight isn't won or lost on the night of the fight. The fight is won with the roadwork. When a guy comes into a fight and he knows he hasn't done the prep work, he's not really totally there. His mind will start to play tricks on him during that fight. That'll work to tire him out, and he'll lose the ability to hold on. If I'd have done everything I could possibly do to prepare for that fight—if I'd have done the roadwork, the practice, the sparring—then I'm gonna go in there with a clear mind and I'm gonna be able to put everything into it. I didn't do enough roadwork."

I think that's a great story, and I've thought of it many, many times since James told it to me. I bring it up again here because the parallel is easy to see: When you haven't done the work, the preparation, the "roadwork," your confidence is easy to shake and you run out of gas. You lose the game because you give up. You lose because you lack confidence. You didn't do the work. Trust me, that does *not* happen to great boxing champions (it didn't happen to De La Hoya that night). It doesn't happen to the greatest of the champions of Wall Street either. If you do the roadwork, you'll have the confidence to see it through.

For me, fundamentals lend themselves to investments in companies I really have a relationship with, and that often leads to private deals. The winners are people intimately involved with the company—people who are committed to it and willing to stand by it forever if necessary.

Many people have become rich this way, and it describes exactly how I feel about the BizRadio Network as well as my capital management company. People may eventually take a public offering of that company (which is not now on the boards), but they may take it just because management has that commitment. People who make passive investments in companies are usually much less committed. They're much less certain about their information, and their belief is more easily shaken—just like a boxer who doesn't do the roadwork.

Cavemen Don't Get Rich

When you bet money, when you invest, especially based on second-hand fundamentals that you learned from someone else, the odds of losing money are very high. Even if what you've been told is correct (which it often isn't), it can take days, weeks, months, and sometimes several years for the effects of the fundamentals to show up in the price of stocks. The longer the timeframe, the more chance there is that some new factor will arise and change everything before your fundamentals have time to make money for you, even if you were right to start with.

Because of this uncertainty, most humans don't have the constitution (or they can't afford) to invest money for their future security or their kids' education, and then sit by for months or even years while their investments lose their value. Their research is incomplete, or they got it from another source without thoroughly checking it out. This weakens their resolve, makes them easy to shake out, and causes them to hang on just enough to sell near the bottom.

So you're wondering how you can be right and lose money? It's easy. When a company whose fundamentals are strong falls in price, other stocks are often falling at the same time. It's happening market-wide. And the move is probably based on some overriding macroeconomic story that you didn't think about when you were evaluating the company. Your herd instinct takes over, and you sell again, most likely and most often near the *very* bottom.

The problem as I've stated it to you is investing based on fundamentals. Here's another variation on the problem. The same facts are known to pretty much everybody, so there's a good chance those fundamentals are already discounted in the price you paid for the investment in the first place. This means that even after you know the fundamentals, you still need just as much market timing, sector analysis, and market x-ray information to make it sensible for you to risk your money as you did when you knew little or nothing about the fundamentals of the company. The bottom line is any information is valuable and fun to know, but to make money betting on fundamentals is a very hard and risky proposition. Most professionals who try it end up broke or, if they're lucky, in another profession.

We are in a time that is way different from the 1980s and 1990s when most Americans started participating in the stock market. Most investors have come through a very frightening roller coaster ride and are permanently affected by the experience. Amateur investors didn't know what to do, because everything they learned in the '90s was a trap. Every action they took burned them.

For the entire bear market of last year, stocks moved only based on supply and demand for the stocks, with no real rhyme or reason. Technical patterns established for years didn't work. Investors in companies that were fundamentally sound suffered exactly the same as investors in terrible companies that can't survive in the long run.

In short, none of the skills people learned over the last 20 years have helped avoid massive losses. Of course most people are punch drunk.

So here's a good rule from a veteran of many campaigns (that's right, me). The more uncertainty in the environment, the more people's herd instinct takes over. As we close out the first decade of the 21st century we've been going through some major political experiments. I personally think there are a lot of bad ideas being floated, but what I think about that isn't really the point. Whether these ideas work out eventually or not, the change breeds uncertainty, and uncertainty paralyzes most people whether they're business people or investors. That paralysis in the face of uncertainty is hardwired into us, and it's another reason we're not naturally adapted well for modern conditions.

You know, when I was thinking about a name for this book, I considered *Cavemen Don't Get Rich*. It's certainly true enough to be one of the subheadlines, because it's a theme that runs through all of our lives from cradle to grave, and mastering our tendencies is the key to success.

Throughout 2009, this government has kept pouring money into the economy like an amateur cook keeps pouring on the charcoal lighter fluid to get the barbecue started. I think the changes and uncertainty the government is creating are actually neutralizing the benefits from all the money they're pouring into it.

The uncertainty is like a wet blanket smothering people's natural tendencies to grow and take risk. The more I see them doing this, the more I want to benefit from betting against them, no matter how well-intentioned the changes are they're proposing. And the harm is often caused by floating these proposals even when they don't actually get passed. They still scare people, still make them feel insecure, still make them defer investment and purchase decisions.

With an impossible number of variables to distract you, the trick is to focus on the few things you know to be true. Here's the truth, even though it is confusing almost everyone.

Long-term viability requires companies to invest in themselves. But in late '08 and throughout '09, CEOs of companies got so pessimistic and so frightened, they stopped investing at all.

No matter how dumb our government's new policies are, and believe me they will turn out to be dumb, some companies are plugged into an economy that's going to grow at 4 percent or 5 percent a year for as far as the eye can see—not the U.S. economy, the world economy. That's as fast as we grew in the United States through the 1990s. Think about it. That was the best time you can remember.

And the companies you know who feed the global growth industry, who help the Asians, Africans, Latin Americans, the Chinese, the Malaysians, the Indonesians, the Brazilians, the companies that feed into their strong growth are the ones that cut payrolls, investment, everything by 90 percent. Even local companies, like national used car dealer Carmax, which are not even about global growth, just about families maintaining and going to work, they're selling cars like hotcakes, but their investment in themselves for 2009 was down by 90 percent. That panic-based frugality isn't going to last. The executives who run companies like Carmax are going to stick their head out of the bomb shelter and get back to work.

Cable company Comcast is concluding its purchase of NBC Universal as I write this. GE is selling off its consumer stuff and investing in global growth, like water purification plants, power plants, and coal gasification. Global industrial inevitable development is exactly the right place to move assets.

Now here's a trick I learned from the very brilliant Tobin Smith years ago:

Instead of buying a huge, diversified, slow-growing conglomerate, such as GE or Exxon, to gain access to those desirable component divisions, why not pick well-run growth companies in each area. You get the well-designed group of diversified positions, but each of them can grow at 20 percent a year or more, instead of 5 percent a year.

That's why we invest in the water business, mentioned elsewhere in this book, instead of just relying on GE. When they get their switching around of assets done, and if we like the combination, we may very well bet on GE. For now, we'll pick fast-growing individual components. With the dollar likely to decline over the next few years, I'm also looking at airplane engine parts manufacturers, again another strong point of GE, a beautiful lifeboat hidden inside a huge unwieldy ship.

I'm sticking my neck out here to make a prediction. You will know whether I was right or not, because you will be reading this book several months after I wrote it. I predict that companies will show, in the last quarter of 2009 and the first quarter of 2010, huge increases in profit because their profits fell off the cliff at the same time a year before. Frightened management cut everything down to zero over the next year. They couldn't do it all at once; it took months of management to cut all that fat, preparing for a depression that never came. And they didn't only cut fat, they cut important muscle as well. So now they have no depression and no investment and drastically reduced expenses. They don't have enough inventories, so they have to build them. More production with much lighter payroll. That will leave people complaining, but companies will be adding to productivity and, more importantly, making profit.

Stop listening to the whining herd and think for yourself.

That's what I'm here for. That's what this book is providing that nobody else does for you.

Think this through. CEOs were scared and hording cash. Banks were frozen in place, and companies were being put out of business. They couldn't raise money, couldn't get loans. Those who could cut expenditures stopped spending on inventories. They cut payrolls. They made it, they survived. But the job of a company in a growth industry is not to hoard cash, it is to build the business, to make investments in growth. We're at the beginning of a global growth cycle—early in it—and you will be shocked at how many companies start to invest in themselves and how much that pushes the American economy.

They'll be doing business overseas, and eventually that's where the growth will be. The American companies with lots of cash that feed global growth—that's where the money will be at first. The investment profits are not going to show up here in the United States for a while.

By the way, I have to clear up another bit of confusion. It's always tough for people who don't know what they're looking at when there are two causes of something. Several years ago there was a problem with our air signal in Dallas, Texas. The engineers diagnosed it, but when they fixed it, the problem didn't go away, and so they put the equipment back the way it was and tried the alternative fix. Again, this didn't work. They were so perplexed.

Now I'm not an engineer, and maybe that's what helped me, because I woke up in the middle of the night and it hit me: Both things are wrong. They were only looking for one solution. That's what happens to linear thinkers.

The truth is, there were two problems.

What does that story have to do with you, here, now?

Well manufacturing has been declining since 2004 and steadily since 2005. Really, we knew long before that that manufacturing wasn't going to be the answer for us, and that cheap foreign labor would be better for manufacturing.

Desperately electing a new president who hasn't got a clue about economics is a last ditch effort to put our collective thumb in the dyke. We cannot hold back the reality that we're going to be bankers, financiers, consultants, and marketing guys, which are the soft, cushy, good-paying jobs anyway, while the rest of the world does the hard, muddy, greasy, sweaty work. So what?

Nothing anybody can do will stop this. The more energy you waste trying to stop it, the poorer you will be. The more energy you put into helping the inevitable come to being, the richer you will get. The bottom line? Wake up. Smell the coffee. Line up with reality and get rich in a world without borders.

As in many of these issues about investing styles and beliefs, you have to figure out what's going to work for *you*. No matter how well you know the fundamentals, in a very uncertain environment the herd instinct remains dominant. Whatever else you consider, you still have to be able to gauge the movements of the herd. If you're going to make money over the next several years, you're gonna have to be even better at it than normal.

Ironically, I find that once I know the mood of the herd (is it stampeding, recklessly buying everything in sight) the rest of it doesn't even matter. It doesn't make much sense to spend too much time learning about the fundamentals of every little company. The big story of our time is that stocks are moving in groups, not by themselves. In the hot areas, there are these horrible, unprofitable companies that will never make any money. They're total scams, and they're doing just as well as excellent companies in the same industries.

The corollary is that great companies don't do any better than mediocre ones in an environment like the one we're in right now because money is flowing into (or out of) groups. You want evidence? Consider this piece of inside information: The worst performing pros are the market-neutral hedge fund operators. Those are the hedge funds that buy a good stock and sell what they think is a bad stock so their total portfolio can be market neutral.

That technique isn't working for a very simple reason: All of the companies in an industry (and basically all of the companies on the stock exchanges) are moving together. They're depending on the emotions of the investors much more than they depend on their own stories, but the real story is about the investors and the herd, not about the investments.

Sure, investing based on your belief in faith and loyalty and certainty about a company is a good way to go, but this means you have to really know about the company. I have lots of my own assets invested in my capital management company, and I never thought to try to sell my stock when the stock market turned down, but this situation is special. I have a great deal to say about the decisions being made, I know the goals and methods of the company, I know its resources, its customers, its sources of revenue, and so forth. I'm not just reading about them and taking advice from strangers. Every day, smart people tell me what they think of as informed ideas and facts about potential investments. Sometimes I actually believe they know what they're talking about, but I never risk one cent on what they say.

Coming Full Circle

All right. Let me remind you again. You are *not* hypnotized. You're completely awake. You're thinking, not just operating on memory cells, so this is a great time to start weighing the advantages and disadvantages of some religious-style beliefs. Rest assured, I mean no disrespect to organized religion, nor do I mean to say that all religious beliefs are wrong. You are Investor 2.0, right? You're determined to avoid (and consciously rise above) beliefs about investing your money that are based on faith in leaders, and the unfounded beliefs of the herd.

Beliefs versus reality on real estate values—do they really rise all the time?

Here's another of those very widespread beliefs—based on absolutely zero factual evidence. It led millions of Investor 1.0 lemmings right over the cliff. Do real estate prices always rise? For some perspective into the all-important U.S. real estate market, take note of the U.S. median price of a single-family home over the past 39 years. Not only did housing prices increase at a rapid rate from 1991 to 2005, there was an increase in the rate at which housing prices increased. But housing prices have dropped 33 percent from the 2005 peak. In fact, a home buyer who bought the median priced single-family home at the 1979 peak has actually seen that home lose value (1.6 percent loss). Not an impressive performance considering that nearly three decades have passed. It's worth noting that the median priced home has moved back to the top of a trading range that existed from the late 1970s into the mid-1990s.

So now we come back to the job we started. To become a rich person who hasn't gotten the money yet, you start with taking full responsibility. You free yourself from habits and belief systems right now. You start with this proclamation: "I have no beliefs." I don't know how much the government meddling in the economy helps or hurts. Neither do the guys on TV who bicker and disagree about it endlessly. I don't know how much to discount for uncertainty, or what to expect from our changing economy and demographics, and neither do the guys on TV who bicker and disagree about it endlessly. My goodness, reader! Do you feel strangely alone or totally liberated?

The Last Word—Danger (The Lemming Spell Comes Back)

Well, I guess it's about time to wrap this up; you and I both have a big day tomorrow. But as you venture out to be a part of this *world without economic borders*, I want to make sure you take all necessary safety precautions. Get your mind in the right mode and make sure you wear your seat belt—the road can get bumpy. Before I see you off, and now that you're totally free for the moment, I have to give you some important (and potentially frightening) news: The tendency to be a lemming keeps coming back. You're seeing life in a way reserved for the very few, and you really aren't built for it. Neither am I. I have to struggle to stay awake, and so will you.

Frankly, my goal is to try to give this understanding and knowledge to my kids, so these skills are so much a part of them that they just come naturally. I haven't figured out how to keep them from reverting when they hit their double digits. Do they get the gift back when they grow out of it? Can't say for sure, but my 20-year-old is showing promising signs. Stay tuned for an update in my next book. For right now, our focus is on our life.

But while you're free, take a look at some of the pressures, influences, and genetic tendencies that have helped get you to where you are right now. You are a being perfectly designed to make terrific decisions when it comes to procreation, but one who must really put in some effort to be good at making money.

Oh yes, it's true. To procreate, you know exactly what to do. I can see it now. If you were hunting for a mate and happened into a bar full of people just like you, you'd get out of there in a hurry. You'd go find a place where the odds are much better. Maybe a place filled with an extraordinarily high ratio of members of the opposite sex—something to boost your odds a little, right?

Now think of your human tendencies as an investor. You feel uncomfortable when you're making an investment move alone, away from the crowd. You'd rather do your investing in a place full to the brim with people exactly like you. Right? It's OK. You can admit all of it. Remember, these are the very natural human tendencies. Now that you're awake, you know you simply have to overcome many of them. So cheer up, you're on your way.

There are a lot of choices for the final few words here. I want to leave you with something inspiring. I want to say something that'll make you feel self-assured, to convince you that your destiny is in your own hands and your limitations are in your own mind. But I'm hoping now that I've already done that in the previous pages.

So, I'll be content to leave you with a thought that just came to me. It put a smile on my face, and as you close the covers of my book, I'd feel fulfilled knowing that you had a smile on your face, too. Here's that final thought.

I never cease to be amused by our human tendency to make the right decisions when it comes to procreation, and to make the wrong decisions when it comes to investing. I'll sleep well knowing that I've helped you to turn the latter around completely, without affecting the former in any way whatsoever.

There. I think that should do it.

About the Author

Who is Daniel Frishberg?

Daniel Frishberg brings us an uncommon sense about money as he shares inside secrets from the front lines of Wall Street. Investment guru, radio and TV personality, author of numerous books, learning courses, newsletters, and other financial publications, Dan Frishberg is the CEO and founder of the Biz Radio Network. In his two-hour daily *MoneyMan Report*, he's created one of the fastest growing sources of information on investing and trading in the country, now reaching audiences all over the United States. In addition to terrestrial AM radio broadcasts in Houston, Dallas/Fort Worth, San Antonio, and Denver, BizRadio is broadcast daily on www.industrialinfo.com. That web site alone brings 30 million hits per month, and Dan's program is regularly picked up on major web sites like Market Wire, Forbes, Dow Jones, and Yahoo! Finance. His stock picks and strategies are reported regularly by thestockadvisor.com, AOL, and MSN.

Daniel Frishberg has become one of the most sought after financial pundits on national TV, appearing often on CNBC, Fox, and the Canadian Business News Network. His commentary is also carried on a rapidly growing number of local TV stations all over the country, while his weekly series "Where Genius Meets Street Smarts" is by far the most downloaded financial podcast on the BizRadio network.

The influence of The BizRadio network on its targeted audience is illustrated by the fact that it has attracted over three quarters of a billion dollars in capital over the past two years, more than half of that in the past twelve months.

His company manages over 300 million dollars in assets, including one of the few equity portfolios in the country that has shown gains over the difficult years of the recent past, more than doubling the S&P 500 performance since its inception in 2001.

Daniel Frishberg is the senior partner of several private equity funds. Along with his associate partners Dr. Arthur Laffer and former mayor David Wallace, he has profitably committed hundreds of millions in capital over the past two years to their real estate, media and other holdings, generating capital at a time when money is considered tight.

Daniel Frishberg's first book *Escape From The Herd* accurately forecasted the current international and domestic market situations. His personal success story is all the more intriguing. He grew up in the 'projects' on the Lower East Side of Manhattan, served as an enlisted Marine Machine Gunner from 1962 to 1965, attended NYU by scholarship, supported himself trading silver contracts, obtained no degrees, and yet has earned countless millions for the many highly educated people who surround him. Daniel Frishberg is a trusted advisor to many of the most famous and respected investors of our time.

Index